REACHING ONE THOUSAND

REACHING ONE THOUSAND

A STORY OF LOVE, MOTHERHOOD & AUTISM

Rachel Robertson

Published by Black Inc.,
an imprint of Schwartz Media Pty Ltd
37–39 Langridge Street
Collingwood Vic 3066 Australia
email: enquiries@blackincbooks.com
http://www.blackincbooks.com

National Library of Australia Cataloguing-in-Publication entry

Robertson, Rachel.

Reaching one thousand : a story of love, motherhood and
autism / Rachel Robertson.

ISBN: 9781863955553 (pbk.)

Includes bibliographical references.

Robertson, Rachel. Mothers of autistic children--Biography.
Autistic children--Biography.

306.8743092

CONTENTS

On Pomegranates and Life Stories:
An Introduction ... 1

Reaching One Thousand ... 7

Raw Experience ... 29

The Blank Face ... 48

Winding ... 65

The Cage ... 80

Bonus ... 94

Geometry of Echoes ... 105

Carving, Forging, Stealing ... 123

Pumpkin Scones ... 140

Frog in Girlland ... 162

Fancy Footwork ... 181

The Shape of a Life ... 203

Acknowledgements ... 213

Notes ... 215

For my son

AUTHOR'S NOTE

The names of all the people in this book (except the author) have been changed in order to help protect their privacy.

In my language use, I have been guided by the writings of autistic people. I use the term 'autistic person' rather than 'person with autism' in acknowledgement that being autistic may be an integral part of a person, not an add-on or something that might be removed or cured. I use the term 'autism', rather than 'autism spectrum disorder', for shorthand. I use the term 'neurotypical' to refer to non-autistic people.

ON POMEGRANATES AND LIFE STORIES: AN INTRODUCTION

The real is not given to us, but put to us by way of a riddle.
—ALBERT EINSTEIN

'I'M HUNGRY FOR SOME FRUIT,' says Ben, standing close beside me so that his arm is on top of my notebook and I have to put down my pen and pay attention to him.

'Okay,' I say, 'let me see what I have.' Ben's always hungry for fruit or salad. In fact his favourite foods are green apples, the stalks of lettuces and tinned pineapple. Today, I have something new for him.

'Look, I bought a pomegranate.'

'Do I like pom-grans?' he asks.

'I don't know, but I expect you will.'

I cut it in two and give him half on a plate with a teaspoon so that he can scoop out the seeds and flesh. He takes it into his bedroom and, from the kitchen, I hear him talking to himself as he eats it. The other half sits skin side up in a bowl on the kitchen bench. I remember many years ago sharing a pomegranate with a man I loved. He read to me from the *Song of Solomon* – 'As a piece of a pomegranate are thy temples within thy locks.' I thought it was romantic. I knew the pomegranate represented fertility, but I didn't know then that the

1

pomegranate is thought by some scholars to have been the forbidden fruit of the Garden of Eden.

I finish making my notes. Then I go into Ben's room.

'How are you going with that pomegranate?' I ask. 'Do you need help getting the seeds out?'

'Yes, please.'

Ben's face is covered with pink juice, his hands and nails are stained red, there are blobs of red all over his Thomas the Tank Engine bedcover, his T-shirt and the floorboards, and a smear of pink on the pale-blue walls. The only clean thing in the room is the teaspoon I gave him. He's managed to dig most of the seeds out with his fingers and then put them into his mouth in clumps.

After Ben has finished the last of the seeds and I've cleaned him and his bedroom up (well, a rough clean, anyhow), he goes outside to swing on a rope from the tree in our garden. This is one of his favourite activities, swinging over the garden, and he likes me to push him. Only he calls it 'a set of pushes', because he wants me to push him five times with differing strengths, starting from 'excellent' – which is actually a small push – moving on through 'good, satisfactory, limited' and ending with 'very low', which is a high, spinning push that has him laughing madly, but never quite letting go of the rope and falling off. This is the way Ben thinks: in ordered sets of a pre-dictable and logical nature. It's just a shame that life and other people are rarely ordered, predictable or logical.

Between swings, Ben runs inside, lifts up the remaining half pomegranate and pokes the seeds.

'Don't touch that, Ben,' I say, not being keen on further mess.

'I'm just admiring it,' he explains. And it is very beautiful, the glistening crimson seeds packed between skin-thin membranes. It's easy to imagine Hades tricking Persephone into eating just a few seeds, thus ensuring her return to the underworld and our winter season. Ben touches it again. 'And besides, it feels strange,' he says.

'Ben, please don't poke it all the time. I've had enough of red drips all over the place. Your fingernails still look like they have blood on them.'

'Speaking of which,' he says, and dashes off into the other room, coming back with a book called *Making Spooky Things at Home* (bought for him by his father, needless to say), 'we could make the frightening foot and horrible hand.'

This is another typical Ben thing: association. The idea of blood made him think of the spooky book. The only thing is, next time he eats pomegranate, he'll want to make something else from the book too, because his mind runs along associational grooves and doesn't vary much. I dig out some black paper and cut hand and foot shapes and then we paste some bone-like strips of white paper over the black paper, creating a skeleton foot and hand. He hangs these on string in his room and tapes a sign over them saying, 'Danger. Frightening foot and horrible hand. Caution.'

Ben loves making signs.

Then he decides to make a list of the different spooky things we could make each day for the next week, so he gathers up paper and pen, sits on the floor and starts writing, his tongue poking slightly out of his mouth as he concentrates.

Ben loves making lists.

It's funny to me now to think of my younger self, equating pomegranate seeds with sexual desire. In fact, I'm wondering if it really was me, or just a dream. (But I know it was me.) Now, when I think of pomegranates, I think of a memoir by Carolyn Polizzotto called *Pomegranate Season*, a book that is partly about her reactions to having a son with a disability. In particular, I think about a wonderful paragraph on the hiatus that the news of a diagnosis can cause. It's such a good passage that the publishers reproduced it on the back cover of the book.

> Loose photographs you can shuffle about. You can pick them up and put them down again in any order you like. Photo albums are for happy families. Children, grown-up, pass them on to their children. When you are thirty-one years old, and the soaring curve of your carefully planned future suddenly freezes into stillness against the sky, photo albums are the first thing to go.

I, too, have a drawer in my desk stuffed full of loose photos. I, too, have photo albums that run from the birth of my son until he is two but then stop. I pretend the desk drawer isn't there; it has a power of its own to open up my insides. Like a fierce animal in a cage, the photos lie untouched, untouchable.

A girl of twenty-something sharing a pomegranate with her lover (where is he now, I wonder?) and the forty-something woman making horror hands and afraid of her bottom drawer – these two people seem unrelated. It seems impossible to remember and connect to the person I was before I had Ben and especially before I realised Ben was different from me, before we gave that difference a name.

Several months ago, I met an old school friend in a supermarket. I recognised her voice first, and turned at the familiar tone. Then we both managed to remember each other's name and that we were at high school together.

'How are you?' she asked.

'Oh, fine, thanks. How are things with you?'

'We're up here for my sons' rowing. You remember I trained to be a teacher?'

I did.

'Well, I got posted to a small country town, met and married a farmer and we have two boys. They're at Guildford Grammar, boarding, you know, doing year eleven and twelve and they're in the rowing team. So we came to Perth to watch them.'

'Oh, lovely,' I said, though I really don't know if watching rowing is lovely.

'And what about you?' she asked.

'Oh, well, um, this is my local supermarket, I live near here. I'm just doing a bit of shopping,' I answered.

Just then, thankfully, the farmer husband appeared and it seemed natural to finish our conversation and wish each other well. Supermarkets always confuse me – too much colour and noise and choice – but even for me, this conversation was vaguer than usual. I was amazed that this woman, whom I hadn't seen for over twenty years, was able to summarise her life since our last meeting in just one minute and to do so in a way that made sense, both to her and to me. She spoke with confidence and warmth. It was easy to guess she adored her husband and children and was very proud of them. I can imagine her sons – two fine, upstanding young men with good complexions and wide shoulders. One would take over the farm and the other do something like teaching or accountancy. I'm sounding bitchy now, which I don't actually feel because this woman was a lovely friend at school and I feel sure that she is a generous and compassionate adult. Still, I can't get over the shock of someone being able to tell their life story so quickly, so easily. If I were to summarise my past twenty-five years, what would I say? I finished my literature degree, went overseas, came back, had three different careers and several failed relationships, had a child, separated from the child's father, ran my own business, gave up the business, started writing a book … It's a mess; it doesn't hold together. It's just a list of things that have happened, not a story.

I might be wrong, but it felt as though my old school friend's one-minute life story actually reflected the fundamentally important aspects of her life and her personality. It wasn't just a recitation of facts; it was a narrative that encapsulated her identity.

My list of things that have happened isn't like that because the narrative that would encapsulate my identity would have to be about Ben and autism. It would have to be the narrative of discovery, reflection and exploration that happens in my head and heart. It's a narrative of detection – who is this boy, my son? Of learning – what does this mean for me, his mother? Of grief – how do I deal with my losses and his losses? And of pleasure – how can I explain the joy he gives me?

This narrative can't be a simple chronological story, though, because my life is one of disruption and disjunction. The 'soaring curve' of an imagined life has been broken and re-made in a different shape. It is earth-bound, not soaring; sharp-edged, not curved. In this, I think, it is actually like most people's stories.

'About the pomegranate I must say nothing, for its story is something of a mystery,' said the second-century Greek traveller and geographer Pausanias. Our life stories are also obscure – to us and to others. We write to try to understand them: even then, they may remain mysterious.

REACHING ONE THOUSAND

I have often admired the mystical way of Pythagoras, and the secret magic of numbers.—SIR THOMAS BROWNE

IN THE KITCHEN OF my mother's houses there has always been a wooden stand with a small notepad and a hole for a pencil. I say small because these notepads are tiny, no bigger than a grown man's palm. The pencils are short and have been sharpened in the same way all these years – with a kitchen knife, not a pencil sharpener – giving them an irregular, squarish lead point.

I'm looking for paper on which to note down the name of a book I am recommending to my mother. Forty-odd years since my earliest memories of the kitchen pad and pencil, five houses later, on a different continent, the current paper and pencil look the same as they always did. Surely it can't be the same pencil? The pad, now I look at it, is more modern than those of my childhood; it is lined and the paper is thicker and creamier. But the grubby wooden stand is definitely the original one, made by my father with the hand tools that sit in a box in my mother's shed.

'I can't believe you still use these scribbly pencils,' I say to my mother, walking back into the living room with a sheet of paper and the pencil. 'Can't you afford a pen?' I flinch as I hear impatience or disapproval in my voice.

My mother replies, a little sharply, 'It works perfectly well.'

'Yes, it does. I'm just amazed you still have the same pad and pencil holder after all these years.'

'Oh yes, I've always kept that in the kitchen. I never knew when I might want to make a note of an idea, and I was always in the kitchen in those days.'

Immediately I can picture her, hair wild, blue housecoat covered in flour, a wooden spoon in one hand, the pencil in another, her mouth moving silently. My mother smiles and says, 'One day I was making shepherd's pie and I had a marvellous thought, but the stand was empty. One of the children must have taken the paper. I was mincing the lamb and boiling potatoes and watching baby Pauline, so I just grabbed the breadboard and wrote it all down on the back. It turned out to be a real breakthrough for solving the problem I was working on.'

This story – which happened before I was born – reminds me how remarkable my mother was, and is. I feel embarrassed that I complain about not having enough child-free time to work. Later, when my mother is in the bathroom, I go into her kitchen and turn over the breadboards (she has three). Sure enough, on the back of the smallest one are some scribbled marks and indentations that I recognise as mathematics. Those symbols have travelled unscathed through fifty years, rooted in the soil of a cheap wooden breadboard, invisible exhibits at every meal.

'Forty-five, forty-three, forty-one.'

'Look, Ben, a cat!'

'That cat lives at number thirty-nine.'

'Maybe.'

'Thirty-seven, mystery, oh, it says number thirty-five on the house.'

Four years ago, Ben and I walked this way almost every day. It was quiet on the streets. It seemed that only Ben loved to visit the dull little park with dirty climbing equipment and wobbly swings.

'Thirty-three, thirty-one, twenty-nine.'

'Look, Ben! Nasturtiums on the verge.' They blossomed with abandon, dark red, orange, yellow, cream with pale red stripes. Huge leaves tipped from side to side in the breeze. 'There are lots of cabbage moths and snails here. If you ever want to find snails, nasturtiums are good for that,' I explained.

'What do I do if I find snails?'

'I don't know, I just mean if you wanted to look at one.'

'Why do I want to look at one?'

'Because they're interesting. Kids like snails.'

'Why do kids like snails?'

'They like to watch them.'

'Why do they like to watch them?'

'Never mind, Ben. What's the next number?'

'Twenty-seven,' he sang joyfully. Oh miraculous discovery, another letterbox, another number.

The park: a small oval of grass, a few trees, a basketball hoop, climbing frame, swing, litter, broken water fountain, sun glinting on flowers.

'Look, Ben – lovely daisies.'

'How many are there?'

'Lots.'

'How many lots?'

'Oh, I don't know, hundreds I guess.'

'I think there are actually eight hundred and forty daisies.'

'Maybe.'

He picked one and counted the petals, then handed it to me before trotting towards the swing.

'Can I swing from one hundred to one?'

'Okay.'

'One hundred, ninety-nine, ninety-eight ...'

Under the swing were woodchips. As I pushed the swing, I saw each chip was a different size and shape. Even the colour varied. My vision narrowed to see details. Like Ben, I could see the difference in sameness.

'Sixty-six, sixty-five, sixty-four ...'

The count went on.

We walked: home and park, home and park, letterbox after letterbox, the only way to keep Ben happy. Pavements, numbers, flowers, weeds, smells of spring embraced us as we passed. The world shrank to the two of us. To the seed pods cracking under our feet, to the blond grass heads haloed in the sun, soft as baby skin. There was no time before now. I had only ever known this – these walks, the pointless looping of feet over earth, days over days, time and again. To dwell within a labyrinth of the mind, of Ben's mind, always circuiting, never arriving. The absence of shared meaning.

When we were young, Olivia and I played a game called 'spot the mathematician'. It started at Heathrow. We were about to fly to Helsinki with our parents for an international mathematical congress, so we knew there would be mathematicians on the plane. As the passengers walked down the gangway, we took it in turns to decide whether they were mathematicians or not.

'He's one,' Liv would whisper. 'Look at his clothes.'

Then it was my turn. 'Look, he sat in the wrong seat – must be one!'

Sometimes we were unsure. 'What do you think, Rachel?' Liv would ask. 'He kind of looks too neat and moves too fast.'

'No, he's not one of ours. He's got a newspaper under his arm.'

We focused on the men, because we knew that our own mother was one of only a small number of female mathematicians. But occasionally we'd see a woman who looked unusual enough for us to consider her a possible candidate. Experience suggested that normal-looking women weren't mathematicians, at least not British ones.

We didn't know much about Finland before we touched down in Helsinki, except that it was the birthplace of the composer Sibelius. At the end of the week's congress we knew little more, just that Finland was famous for cloudberries. While our parents attended conference talks, we went on the 'wives and children' tours. We were used to this and usually managed to attach ourselves to some kindly woman who would keep an eye on us and make sure we got lunch. This was what my mother would say to me each morning as she left the motel room: 'Be good, look after Olivia and make sure you both get a good lunch.'

It was at the congress dinner that Liv and I perfected our maths stereotype. As soon as the food arrived, it seemed that every mathematician made a mad beeline for the buffet tables and grabbed all he could. It was the first time all week we'd seen them stop talking. From then on, a type of animal hunger was added to our list of characteristic mathematical traits.

Overheard, a boy talking to his older sister:

'Look, there's that boy Ben from school I told you about. He knows all the times tables and he's only in year one!'

Although my mother was a gifted and successful mathematician, it never crossed my mind that I would follow in her footsteps.

From an early age, I had a clear sense that I was in some way fundamentally different from both of my parents and that mathematical ability was one of the key markers of this difference. As a child I felt as though I was outside an invisibly marked space and was without knowledge of the key that would permit me to enter it. I felt that at least two of my siblings had the ability to slip in and out of this place, because at times they seemed to understand what my parents meant. Of course, I understood the words my parents spoke, but it seemed that the unspoken meanings were lost on me. As I became older and more critical, I began to realise that my parents weren't 'ordinary'. My difference from them became a matter of being ordinary, not odd. Right into my twenties, I naïvely held on to this dichotomy of odd versus ordinary, mathematical versus non-mathematical, and (perhaps without really realising it) intelligent (them) versus stupid (me). Even after I moved on from this simplistic view, mathematics still functioned as the symbol of my difference from my parents.

And then I had Ben.

'You need to deal with his stimming now, before it gets worse.' The psychologist was young and definite.

I wanted to say: don't tell me what to do. Instead, I said, 'We don't use the terms "stimming" or "obsession". We think of numbers as a strong interest of Ben's.'

'Yes, of course,' she said. 'But would you say that Ben's *interest* in numbers is preventing him being interested in other things, in people, in learning other games and so on?'

'He's not interested in other things, no.'

'So ...' I could hear a slight triumph in her tone and felt sure she didn't like me much. 'Let's talk about how we can reduce the number obs— interest.'

This was when she explained our options: extinguishment, quarantine or integration. It didn't seem to strike her that the words themselves made this seem like a punishment. The choices boiled down to: forbid Ben access to numbers (how, I wondered?); limit his access; or turn his interest into something more 'functional'. The thing was that I agreed with her, but I couldn't bear to remove from Ben his life-blood, the only meaningful thing in his world.

'But numbers aren't meaningful, are they?' she said.

Overheard, one sister talking to another:

'I know, I do exactly the same. I count the steps of every stairway; I count every slice I make when I cut up a banana; I always notice car number plates and bus numbers. I've always done it.'

One of our delights as children was to play with five boxes of buttons my mother kept in her sewing cupboard. They were mostly old chocolate boxes made of tin with pictures of fluffy cats and idealised dogs on them. Each one was full of buttons that we could tip onto the floor. The five boxes were graduated by size, which corresponded to the size of the buttons inside. The largest box contained the largest buttons and so on. I liked the smallest, a white cardboard box with flowers on it that still smelt faintly of something sweet and slightly exotic – vanilla perhaps. In this box there was a cute ladybird button, a brass squirrel and several transparent buttons that were curled up into cylinders like people did with their tongues for fun. These were my favourites. I loved the feel of the buttons running through my fingers when I tipped them from hand to hand or placed them inside their square white home.

It was a surprise to see the button boxes again one day when Ben and I visited my mother. I hadn't realised she had kept them.

'Children love buttons,' said my mother. She was right; even Ben got interested in them. He was four years old at the time and we were struggling to find anything that would amuse him. He certainly didn't play like other children. But the buttons were perfect for him, because he could lay them out on the rug, grouping them by size or colour and matching any that looked the same. He understood the size distinctions, too. He even made my mother label each box with a number, so that the largest buttons were in box one and the smallest in box five. Strangely, he too liked the transparent tongue-curl buttons best.

I remember that visit to my mother well, because after Ben had finished with the buttons, my mother found several other activities for him: smelling each of her perfume bottles, counting and reading the names on her long row of herb and spice jars, placing a single soft toy on each of her wooden steps (this made me nervous because of the gaps between each step and Ben's soft, floppy body) and finally banging away on the piano and learning the name of each note. As my mother and I sat drinking tea to the sound of the piano-bashing, we were both in awe, me of my mother's ability to amuse Ben and her of Ben's intelligence and memory.

'He can read all those spice jars,' she said. 'He even remembered "cardamom" and words like that. Has he seen those at home?'

'Ah, no.' The idea of me managing to cook with spices at that stage of my life was laughable.

'He understands size and categories with the buttons. And he seems quite musical.'

'Maybe.'

Personally I didn't think that hitting random keys of the piano constituted musicality but I guessed that my mother – like me – was still coming to terms with the idea of Ben being autistic. She wanted to focus on his abilities, not his disabilities.

Then my mother said, 'You know, Rachel, you can't really call Ben handicapped. He just has a very particular genetic inheritance.'

When my parents talked about mathematics they often stood in the kitchen. Or rather, my mother moved around preparing dinner, and my father bounced up and down on a small square of floor in front of the most useful cupboard. As they talked about quadratic equations or topological vector spaces, my mother would gently push my father to one side so that she could reach inside the cupboard, and after she had closed the cupboard, he would hop back in front of it. If he was only mildly excited or interested, he would just do his hop, balancing first on his right foot and then moving the left beside it for a quickstep before moving back to the left again. If the conversation was going well, my father would occasionally tap his forehead with the back of his right hand. When things heated up, he would add a left-handed slap to the back of his head just before the right hand hit the forehead, creating a kind of chain reaction. As the dinner neared preparation, there would be a flurry of activity in that kitchen, my mother stirring pots and lifting things out of the oven (she was feeding seven every night), and my father bouncing and hopping, slapping and tapping. Just when the conversation and the dinner were reaching a head, my mother would dash out into the passage and ring an old cow's bell she'd picked up in Switzerland, and one of us kids would dart into the kitchen, dodging wordlessly between my parents to collect the cutlery to set the dining-room table. A few minutes later, the bell would go again, signalling time to eat and a temporary end to the mathematical dialogue.

*

There is a game that some parents of autistic children play, where they try to determine from which side of the family the autism has come. This family blame game is an alternative to the vaccination, birth-trauma or toxic-chemical blame routines. One mother I met told me that she felt guilty because the autism must have come from her family; she had a cousin with autism and her husband didn't know of any autistic people in his family.

'But does it matter? I mean, do you need to know, even if you could?' I asked her.

'I feel bad,' she said. 'If it wasn't for me, my husband could have had a normal child.'

Robert and I have never played this game. I didn't see the need to find or create a 'reason' for Ben being who he is. Nonetheless, it's hard to escape noticing aspects of my own family's behaviour that verges on the autistic spectrum. In one of the first books about autism I read – a book full of depressing statistics and unwelcome generalisations – I saw the sentence: 'The presence of odd family members ... as well as very mathematically bright but socially awkward relatives, is more frequent in families with an autistic child.' I also distinctly remember reading and telling Robert that of all parental occupations, the coupling with the statistically highest likelihood of having a child or grandchild with autism is that of two mathematicians. I remember reading this – even the shape of the print on the page – but now I can't find the reference anywhere. Did I make it up? Did I need a reason for Ben's autism, after all? Even if I did make this up, I know now that it is roughly accurate, because research has shown that mathematicians have a higher rate of autistic-spectrum conditions than the general population, and that the parents and grandparents of children with autistic spectrum conditions are twice as likely to work as scientists, mathematicians and engineers than the parents or grand-parents of non-autistic children.

When I suggested to my sister Megan that perhaps our father (who died before Ben was born) had a few mild autistic-like traits, she said, 'No, he wasn't like that.'

'Wasn't he?' I asked. 'I always thought him a little unusual.'

'Oh no,' she replied, quite upset, 'I don't think of him that way at all.'

I changed the subject. I didn't say to her that the thought of something of my father travelling through me to my son was a comfort to me, a feeling that Ben is not such an outsider in the world after all.

Ben's love of numbers is both mystical and pedestrian. It is unrelenting and ever-present. Not a day goes by when he doesn't count or talk about or write down numbers. The American diagnostic bible on 'mental disorders', the *Diagnostic and Statistical Manual of Mental Disorders*, or *DSM IV*, describes Ben's love of numbers as 'a preoccupation with a stereotyped and restricted pattern of interest that is abnormal in intensity and focus'. Psychologists have described his behaviour as 'obsessional', 'compulsive' and 'ritualised'. I prefer to call him passionate.

What can it mean to have a passion for numbers? Mainly, Ben just loves the physical shape and form of them. Whatever size or colour or font or material a number is made of or written in, he dotes on zero to nine, just as I adore every inch of his body, every expression of his face.

This is how Ben's passion started. Some time before he was two, I stuck on the wall a child's poster with the numbers one to twenty and illustrations to match. I put it up because it was colourful and the hallway was dingy. I read it to Ben once.

He spent a long time looking at it that day, and the next day, and the day after. Then he wanted to 'hold' the numbers. So I made some numbers out of coloured pipe cleaners. These became his most treasured possessions. He laid them down on the floor one after another, saying the numbers as he did, 'one, two, three', and so on up to twenty. Then he started going beyond twenty. When he came to numbers requiring two of the same digit, like twenty-two, he used his hand for the second number. How did he know how to count beyond twenty? This I don't know. It seemed to be innate. A two-year-old unable to eat with a spoon, uninterested in toys, and calling himself 'you' instead of 'I' was able to count to one hundred and beyond. His face was rapt when he used the pipe cleaners for this purpose. He laid them down with such reverence it was like a form of worship. He was so content I could have gazed at his counting face for hours.

After the pipe cleaners, Ben discovered the joys of birthday-cake candles shaped like numbers. But they broke too easily when he played with them, so we found plastic magnetic numbers in a toyshop. He collected handwritten numbers on paper, numbers cut from wrapping paper, golden cardboard numbers, a set of metal numbers from the hardware store intended to be used on letterboxes, numbers for use in the bath, numbers made of playdough, shells that 'could be a six or upside down could be a nine'. And so it went, a cupboard full of sets of numbers, as if collecting the objects was the sole purpose of his life.

Over a period of months, Ben's interest developed. He began to love numbers in a second way, for what they represented, just as a mother will love best the photographs of her children that remind her of happy times. He loved that numbers on letter-boxes tell us the number of the house, that the age we are tells who is older than whom, that numbers can represent so many different things – weight, height, currency, size. Clocks, calculators, thermometers and measuring tapes were all added to his collection.

'He'll grow out of it,' my friends told me.

'He's so intelligent,' my family said.

'Your parents are mathematicians,' people reminded me. 'What did you expect?'

What did I expect? We expect many things of our children. Most of the time we are only aware of these expectations when something happens to make it impossible for them to be fulfilled.

Just as Robert and I were thinking that we should start to teach Ben arithmetic, he found it for himself. He discovered a third way to enjoy numbers: the way they work. That one plus one equals two and then two plus one equals three made sense to him. He began to do strange feats of simple arithmetic. He spent hours adding numbers in his head. 'Two plus two is four; four plus four is eight; forty-four plus forty-four is eighty-eight.'

Soon after that, I would hear him reciting the times tables to himself in bed at six in the morning, starting with 'one two is two' and ending with 'twelve twelves are one hundred and forty-four', complete with the intonation and accent from Don Spencer's musical times-tables CD, which I had foolishly played to him. This may have led him to a fourth way of loving numbers – as an ordering principle. Numbers are predictable and controllable and they never end. He realises you can count forever.

At several points in my schooling I began to fail maths tests. At first I kept it a secret, but after a short while my mother magically knew I was struggling. I don't know if she recognised my failing-maths shame or if my teachers or one of my siblings told her.

At any rate, she would choose a time when we were alone together (a fairly rare occurrence in my family) and ask me how I was going with my maths and was there anything I wanted to tell her. I soon realised that this was the cue to get my maths book and show her my latest test results. She would then put aside some time to work with me on my homework.

'It's just a matter of understanding it,' she would say. 'Once I explain it and you concentrate, it'll be easy.'

In this way, my mother was an optimist. She was an optimist through long division, the change over to decimal currency, geometry and the angle of the hypotenuse, introduction to algebra and, finally, logarithms. She was an optimist, but frustrated.

'For goodness sake, Rachel, you're just not trying!' she would say in exasperation. She couldn't understand how I could appear to take in what she was telling me and answer a couple of questions correctly but then show no ability to apply this knowledge to other similar problems. Nor could she believe that I would forget information within half an hour of her giving it to me, so that every maths session seemed completely new and newly difficult.

We struggled on, both hating it and both counting the days until I finished school and would never have to open another maths text. When my school leaving exam results came out, I was amazed to find I had scored a B in maths. I was bracing myself for a fail or, at best, a C. My mother, however, was disappointed, saying, 'You could have done much better if you'd made up your mind to make the effort.' I looked at her in astonishment; all these years and she still hadn't realised – I didn't understand a single thing. I had just learned how to move rows of incomprehensible numbers and letters from my head into the right spaces on the page. It was like walking through an unknown landscape covered in a thick, suffocating fog. If I stumbled upon my destination, it was purely by chance. My mother's tutorials over the years were simply a wayward breeze, shifting the fog just for a moment before it settled back down for life.

Robert and I finally agreed to 'quarantine' Ben's numbers. But instead of limiting him to using them once a day, we did the reverse: he was not allowed to talk about numbers at dinner.

'Why can I not talk about numbers at dinner?' Ben asked yet again.

'Remember we talked about it. Not everyone finds numbers as interesting as you do.'

'Why not?'

I didn't really know how to answer that one.

'Let's talk about our day,' suggested Robert. 'What did you two do after kindy this afternoon?'

'We went to the park, didn't we, Ben?' I said.

'Yes. First we passed number forty-one, then we passed number thirty-nine …'

'Stop!' I said, rather loudly, holding up the palm of my hand. 'No numbers.'

Robert put his hand over his mouth.

'I know what else happened,' I added hurriedly. 'Auntie Liv rang, didn't she, Ben?'

'Yes.'

'Ben talked to her for a bit, didn't you?'

'How old is Auntie Liv?' asked Ben.

'Ben, you know she's thirty-nine,' I replied.

'Mum is forty-one. Daddy is fifty-five. Auntie Liv is thirty-nine. Granny is …'

'Ben – enough! No numbers at dinner.'

Ben put on his hurt face. 'I don't want any more.'

'Finish your dinner, please.'

'No, I don't want to.'

'You need to eat proper food. Just have four more spoonfuls of rice and then you can get down,' I said.

'One, two, three, four,' he chanted, stuffing them all into his mouth at once and then looking like a cartoon character, cheeks so bunched up he couldn't chew.

'That went well,' said Robert in his dry way. I started to laugh. Ben watched me for a bit and then opened his mouth so that all the rice came spurting out onto the tabletop. He jumped off his chair and ran into his bedroom shouting, 'One, two, three, four. One, two, three, four.'

Robert peered at the bits of rice in his red wine and then drank it. 'He's a clever little fellow, isn't he?' he said proudly.

Overheard, Ben to his teacher:

'Actually, you are wrong: today is the sixteenth, not the fifteenth.'

I wanted to understand why Ben was so obsessed with numbers. Our paediatrician said that obsessions like this were just part of the condition of autism and that it was probably a way for Ben to create order and structure in his life. This sounded a bit vague to me, so I did some more of my (obsessive?) reading about autism. Several months and about twenty books later, I decided that the paediatrician had made a fairly good summary of the situation.

'I should hope so,' said Robert. 'That's why we pay so much to see him.'

But it seems to me that researchers don't really know why people with autism fixate on particular obsessions, only that they will have at least one area of obsessive repetition, whether this is flapping their hands, touching the corners of doors, learning all there is to know about trains or insects, memorising phone books or simply running sand through their hands all day. It is partly a retreat to the concrete because it is so difficult for someone with autism to understand other people and abstract ideas. Repetition is also a way of regulating sensory stimulation, of dealing with sensory overload and high anxiety. The repetition helps calm and regulate.

It has also been suggested that people with autism focus on small details because they lack the ability to see 'the big picture', to integrate things and make sense of the world. Their ability to shift attention is also impaired – it's hard to move on from one thing to the next, hence the desire for sameness.

The most recent theory about autism is that it is an extreme form of the 'male' or systematising brain. Our brains are made to understand systems and how physical objects work, but some people have an extreme ability to understand 'folk physics'. This comes at a cost: their ability to understand people may be limited.

But why numbers? Numbers are a common interest for people with autism. I wanted to know if there was a reason for this.

'Why do you need a reason?' asked Robert. 'Why can't you accept Ben as he is?'

'I do accept him. I just want to understand.'

'What's to understand, Rachel? He likes numbers.'

Overheard, my mother talking to my brother:

'Today is a very special day for me. Today, Olivia is exactly half my age.'

'She has been all year, hasn't she? Or, do you mean half your age to the day?'

'Of course! It wouldn't mean anything otherwise.'

*

Ben's world, like that of most people with autism, is full of confusion, uncertainty and unpredictability. This is partly because of his difficulty in understanding other people and partly because he experiences every object, every person, every thought as a separate unique event, with no necessary or logical connection to any other event. What is it like to see each tree as an individual as different from another tree as it is from a car, a dog or a man? In a way, it is a vision of total equality. All things are equal; no one, nothing, is elevated. All sense of meaning fails because how can we create meaning without metaphor, categories and hierarchies? Without taxonomy we have chaos, just unmediated, inexplicable experience. The world presses upon us. Our own bodies press upon us. There is no sense to be made of sensation. This is Ben's world – one of experience and perceptions without order, definition or explanation. Could this be anything other than frightening?

It is impossibly hard for a non-autistic person to see, hear and feel the world in the way an autistic person might. Even listening to someone with autism is not enough, because the shared language is always our language, the words and concepts and structures of the neurotypical world. Is there a 'language' of autism, a language for undifferentiated experience?

How can one survive in such a world? You would have to escape, to shut down. Or you could create a structure to manage it all. For Ben, numbers are true to the etymology of the word integer: 'whole, entire' and 'marked by moral integrity'.

Did Ben choose numbers or is it simply that numbers (arithmetic and geometry) form one of the basic underpinning concepts of nature? Spiders spin webs in logarithmic progression. Shells grow in the same proportion. The structure of a snowflake is fractal. Many plants grow according to the Fibonacci sequence of numbers. Our bodies, our landscape, our architecture, our music are all structured according to mathematical principles. Evidence for the human capacity for counting goes back more than thirty thousand years to signs of tallying on bone and on the walls of Upper Palaeolithic caves. In missing the big picture, Ben has perhaps been able to see and appreciate what psychologist Peter Szatmari calls 'the intimate architecture of the world'.

Overheard, Robert talking to Ben:

'Look, Ben, here is the value of phi – you remember, that's Greek and it's the same as the golden mean.'

'Why is it mean?'

'No, not mean like horrid. It's a maths word – the golden ratio. I'll show you in this book about Pythagoras.'

Daniel Tammet is a young man with Asperger's Syndrome who is also a savant with extraordinary mathematical and linguistic skills. In his book *Born on a Blue Day*, he says about numbers:

There are moments, as I'm falling into sleep at night, that my mind fills suddenly with bright light and all I can see are numbers – hundreds, thousands of them – swimming rapidly over my eyes. The experience is beautiful and soothing to me. Some nights, when I'm having difficulty falling asleep, I imagine myself walking around my numerical landscapes. Then I feel safe and happy. I never feel lost, because the prime number shapes act as signposts.

I love this passage because it gives me some sense of how Ben might feel about numbers. Since Tammet has synaesthesia (a neurological difference in which the senses are mixed), his vision of numbers is extremely unusual, much more colourful and textured than most people's. But perhaps Ben also has reassuring visions of numbers. When I asked him if he sees numbers inside his head, he went and stood in front of the mirror and said, 'Where are they? I can't see them.'

Ben's latest interest is prime numbers. He understands that prime numbers are not divisible by any numbers other than one and themselves and that they occur irregularly. He will often interrupt an activity with a comment or question to me such as, 'Mum, is eight hundred and sixty-three a prime number?' or 'Mum, that house is one hundred and seventy-nine; it's a prime number.'

He has also made up his own series of numbers, which he has named 'sweb' numbers. I have yet to discover the clue to this series; they appear to be random and varying. Is it a random series of numbers that Ben believes have some continuity, or just a list of numbers that he likes? Or is it a random series that he knows to be random and is just using for his own interest (or as a joke)? Last week when I went to collect Ben from Megan's house, I found her husband sitting at his computer.

'Ah, Rachel,' he said. 'You can tell us how to spell sweb. Is it German or something?'

'Um ... did you ask Ben?'

'He won't say. But I'm trying to find out about these sweb numbers and there doesn't seem to be anything on the net. If you look up prime numbers, there are heaps of sites.'

It was only at this point that I realised that he wondered if sweb numbers were a genuine mathematical curiosity, not just some game of Ben's. That night on the phone I told my mother the story.

'Sweb numbers,' she said, a little hesitantly. 'Should I know about those?'

'Of course not. Ben just made them up. That's the point.'

'Oh, I see.' But I could tell she didn't see.

'Am I the only person who finds this funny?' I asked Robert, somewhat rhetorically. 'What's the matter with my family – can't they see it's a bit odd to take a seven-year-old's word on maths?'

Robert smiled his tolerant-with-Rachel smile.

I wake to the sounds of objects being moved around in Ben's room: the dragging of his rug across the wooden floor, the soft crush of a beanbag hitting something hard, and then a loud crash, as if a box of toys has tipped over.

'Ben, what are you doing?' I call out, not wanting to get up yet. He comes into my room, a worried look on his face.

'Are you cross?'

'No, darling. I just want to know what you're up to.'

'I'm making space in my room,' he explains.

'Oh. For what?'

'I'm going to have a thousand things in my room. I need more space.'

'One thousand!' I sit up in bed and put on my glasses.

'Am I allowed to?' he asks anxiously.

'Yes, I guess so.' I'm a bit hesitant. 'But isn't a thousand an awful lot of things? I mean, is there space? Do we have a thousand things? Could you even keep count?'

His face clears. 'It's okay,' he says happily, 'I'm going to have ten rows of one hundred things. That will make a thousand, won't it?' And off he goes, back to his arrangements.

Two hours later, when we have to leave for school, Ben has finished his first row of one hundred objects, consisting of thirty-two marbles, fifteen Thomas the Tank Engines, sixteen coloured pencils, a stack of CDs (eighteen), a packet of tea bags (ten), six toy dinosaurs and three odd socks.

27

'Goodness me!' I say. 'What a lot of work you've done.'

'But I've only done one row,' says Ben. 'Do we really have to go now?'

'Yes, we really have to go now. You can come back to this after school. If you still want to, that is. You might decide that one hundred is enough after all.'

'I might,' says Ben, 'but I might still want to reach one thousand!'

RAW EXPERIENCE

What sweet Contentments doth the Soul enjoy by the Senses? They are the Gates and Windows of its Knowledge, the Organs of its Delight.—WILLIAM DRUMMOND

'JUST GIVE IT A TRY, Ben.'

'You don't want to.'

'Ben, just try it, please.' I lift him up and try to put him into the plastic yellow swing that we've hung under the carport. He struggles, kicking his legs, 'You don't want, you don't want.' I dump him into the seat, pull the leg guard down and buckle him in.

'Just try it.' I'm getting a bit irritated now. He's two years old. Every two-year-old likes swinging. 'Now,' I say, and gently push the swing. He's crying, not hard, just a little. So I keep going and start singing a song, 'Swing low, sweet Benji-o.' He stops crying but still looks unhappy. After one verse of the song, he reaches out his arms, saying, 'You want to get down.' He isn't enjoying himself. I stop the swing and lift him out. I'm shocked to feel his heart beating madly against my neck as I cuddle him, his arms grabbing my hair as if it's a lifeline.

'You don't like,' he repeats several times.

'I understand,' I tell him. 'Let's go do something else.'

But I don't understand. Why wouldn't he like swinging?

'I know,' I say. 'Let's make mud pies.' All kids like that, don't they? I get a bowl of water and carry it to the sand patch.

'Here, Ben, take the trowel and put some sand in the water.' I show him how to do it then give him the trowel. But he can't seem to scoop up any sand. I put my hand over his and do it with him. Then, instead of turning the trowel upside down to tip it out, he drops the whole lot, sand and trowel, into the bowl.

'Never mind, that's okay.'

When we've put lots of sand into the water, I mix it up and then take a handful and make it into a ball. 'Would you like a cake, sir?' I ask. Ben stares at me.

'It's a pretend cake,' I explain. 'You make one now.' I put some wet sand into his hands. He drops it immediately and wipes his hands on his T-shirt.

'You don't like,' he says, his face blank. He gets up and walks away.

It's 10.30 in the morning. We have a whole day to fill. I've tried kid's television, hide and seek, and playing with soft toys. He isn't interested.

'Let's play inside, Ben,' I suggest. He follows me into the house.

'How about we make a cave?' I suggest. 'Would you like a cave, Ben?'

'Yes.'

'Okay, here we go.' I move some chairs together and put a large blue blanket over the top. Then I put some cushions on the floor and we climb inside. We sit together in the half-light.

'We need a torch, don't we? You stay here and I'll get one.'

When I return with the torch, the cave is no more. Instead, Ben is lying under two cushions, a blanket and a toppled chair.

'Ben, are you okay? What happened?'

He doesn't reply, but he's smiling. The weight of the chair on his body seems to please him. I move the chair and lie next to him, hugging him. He rolls so that he is almost under my body, and I realise that he is relaxed now in a way he hasn't been all morning. We lie there in our broken cave and he is happy.

Why didn't Ben like swinging, I wondered? Why did he love heavy weights on his body? Why was he happy to spend hours arranging different flavoured herbal tea bags in a row, smelling them and then rearranging them, but did not want to play with his four colourful teddy bears? There were so many puzzling moments like this with Ben. He was sensitive to noises – even a sneeze frightened him. He was always placing his hands over his ears. He hated touching certain things and if he got food on his face or hands, he'd freak out. Although he loved party pies, he wouldn't eat one unless I carefully spoon-fed him and made sure not a single drop of meat or gravy touched his face. Having a haircut was agony for him: the sound of the scissors terrified him and the feel of any cut hair on his cheek would cause him to run around madly, rubbing and rubbing his face. He was funny about certain foods, too; things like jelly and egg made him gag when they touched his tongue. Once we walked into a building early in the morning and he started gagging, pointing to his mouth, saying, 'Get it out, get it out.' It took me several minutes to realise that the smell of cleaning fluid was so strong he could taste it. And, just as noisy places distressed him, so, too, did anywhere with lots of visual stimulation. He would get confused very quickly and fall into a blank, silent state, as if he wasn't 'there' any more.

Between the ages of eighteen and thirty months, the number of things we could do with Ben dropped radically. In the space of a year, we stopped swimming lessons, gym classes, play group, going to the supermarket, sending him to day care, visiting friends with children, attending birthday parties or going to any place where there would be more than about four other people. There were fewer and fewer places we could take him and fewer and fewer things he seemed to want to do. Sometimes even the local park was too much for him and he would loll against my body, exhausted by ten minutes on the play equipment, as I half dragged, half carried him back home.

It took me a long time to realise that these reactions were to do with sensory integration. In fact, it wasn't until I met Alison, occupational therapist extraordinaire, that I understood that Ben's sensory system wasn't functioning effectively. Sensory integration is the normal neurological process of organising our sensations for use in everyday life. Our brain receives sensory information from our bodies and surroundings, interprets this information and organises our purposeful responses. What Alison showed me was that Ben's brain processed sensory messages in ineffective ways, resulting in difficulties with everyday activities. When he was swinging, Ben's body was unable to tell him where he was or what was happening to him. Instead, it was as though he was flying off the earth without any control or predictability and with a feeling like vertigo. No wonder he hated it.

It is now known that almost all people with autism experience some form of sensory integration or processing difficulty. Their experiences of sensory input and ability to process and make sense of this input are profoundly different from the experiences of neurotypical people. The extent of this difference is hard to explain and imagine but it is sometimes likened to a faulty volume knob on a sound system – suddenly you are flooded with unbearable amounts of sensory input of all kinds and you can't sort or separate any of it into manageable information.

People with autism may be over-sensitive or under-sensitive in their perception of some or all of the senses and some people move between over- and under-sensitivity. In addition to this, the way this sensory information is processed by the brain varies, so that making sense of sensory input is very challenging. Auditory processing problems are one reason many autistic children struggle with language. Ben was unusual in that his auditory processing seemed quite good. But his visual processing was different. He would often struggle to make sense of what he saw: he couldn't distinguish foreground from background and seemed to see the world in two dimensions. He once said to me, 'Why is that cat walking into the tree?' I tried to explain that the cat was walking behind the tree and then pointed out that the cat had re-appeared the other side of the tree's trunk. He said, 'It got out.' He couldn't visualise distant space as three-dimensional.

When our senses misfire like this, it affects a whole range of other development. In her book *The World of the Autistic Child*, psychologist Bryna Siegel explains how our sensory systems respond to stimuli from the outside world and represent this information as patterns of neural firing that serve as mental models or schemata. We need these mental models to interpret present experiences and anticipate future ones. They help us generalise and make the world familiar and manageable. Siegel suggests that without effective multi-sense mental models, we would have to learn anew with every experience. The use of sensory systems to create mental models is a building block of development. It starts from birth and is essential to a child's growth and learning. Motor skills, coordination, imagination, emotional regulation and abstract thought all rely on effective sensory modulation and processing.

Looking back to my early childhood, what I remember most are lots of small moments of fear. Walking alongside Olivia on the road to school – the terrible roar of passing trucks (we called them lorries then), the sickening smell of leaded petrol and diesel, the small *thwump* as large vehicles passed us, the in-suck of air in their wake.

The teachers and children at school, the noise and confusion of so many people in a small space. How individuals seemed to merge into a mass of unknown faces and voices. The frightening expectation that I would talk to other children, play with them, trust them.

Stepping outside the house and fearing trees. Keeping my head low, not daring to look up at the tall trunk and branches. Only going outside if I was with someone else. The terrible dizziness of looking up and seeing twigs and leaves against the clouds, my heart like a trapped animal inside, waiting for the tree to fall on me.

Fear around animals – watching Olivia feed the horses through the gap in the fence, their thick lips pulling away from their yellowy teeth as they ate. The swans on the bank of the river, knowing that a swan could break a child's arm in its beak, pulling Liv away as they hissed towards us.

The anxiety of having to touch certain things – soft, pliable or messy things. The feeling of revulsion if I had to touch paint or soft dough or mud, the relief of washing.

Is this what everyone remembers? Do we only remember the frightening sensory experiences of our childhoods? Or is it that my fearful nature meant I experienced more anxiety than other children?

'You were like a little mouse,' says my mother. 'For years you barely strayed from my side, and then when we sent you to nursery school at four years old, what a fuss! Luckily you took to the teacher – I can't remember her name, but she was a nice woman. Very understanding.'

I remember that, too. The metal gate with diagonal silver mesh, a crazy-paving path, edged by grass. My mother's hand, cool, slightly brown, the veins prominent and blue, two dark brown moles, one with a black hair. My mother's hand as she struggles to pull it out of my tight grip, her other hand, pushing at the back of my neck, a voice high above my head, 'Go on, Rachel, go on!' Down the crazy paving, eyes on every crack, over the muddy gap, past the lone forget-me-not plant, on towards the classroom. Indistinct noise and bright light bouncing all around me, assaulting me. Eyes speeding from place to place, looking for the legs. There they are: two thin legs in beige stockings wrinkled around the ankles. Below them brown lace-ups, above a brown tweed skirt, one thread loose. And a hand, this one bony, with long white fingers, nails cut square, the flesh under them pink and delicate looking. This hand is warm and dry and squeezes my hand once before cradling it gently. But even this hand won't stay with me. Soon, too soon, my fingers are softly unpeeled and the hands hold my shoulders before pressing me into a small chair. Once again, I am alone in a sea of strangers.

'Why do you think I was so anxious?' I ask my mother.

'I don't know, dear, that's just how you were. Cautious.'

In the West, we identify five senses – vision, hearing, touch, taste and smell. But this categorisation is a cultural construction. In Buddhist cultures, the mind is a sixth sense. In Nigeria, the Hausa have only two senses – vision and the rest.

In recent years, scientists have identified other senses. Touch has been broken down into kinaesthesia (our sense of movement), perception of temperature and perception of pain. The vestibular sense tells us our position in space (movement, gravity, head position) and the proprioceptive sense gives us an unconscious awareness of the body's position, through muscles, tendons, joints and connective tissue. In her book *Worlds of Sense*, Constance Classen notes that babies have been shown to orient themselves by sonar, emitting and responding to sounds bouncing off walls, like bats. Humans have also been shown to have a rudimentary sense of magnetism, able to distinguish between magnetic north and south.

Classen traces how vision became the sense of primary importance in the West from the Enlightenment onwards. The cultural shift from smell to vision, she argues, was bound up with the decline of myth, community and domestic manufacture and the rise of empiricism, individualism and industrialisation. She claims that whereas smell is concerned with essences, sight reveals surfaces, the sensory shift reflecting different conceptual models. It's an appealing theory.

In parts of India, smelling the head is a traditional form of greeting, a way of filling oneself with the presence of the other. I think Ben would like to greet others like this. In fact, he often does smell my body, as if re-acquainting himself with me. The other day, Laura and her two children came to dinner. After eating, Mel and Joe decided to have a bath and put on their pyjamas, so that if they fell asleep in the car driving home, Laura could put them straight into bed. After their bath, I offered to read to all three children. Ben and Mel sat next to me on the sofa and Joe perched on the arm. As I opened the book, I saw Ben carefully sniff Mel before relaxing against me. Mel looked at him in some alarm.

'Does Mel smell nice after her bath?' I asked Ben.

'Yes,' replied Ben and Mel smiled.

Later I said to Ben, 'It's probably not a good idea to smell people like that. They might not like it.'

'Why not?'

'Well, they might think you're suggesting they smell bad,' I explained. Ben stared at me for a moment, a look of incomprehension on his face. But only for a moment; then I could see him give up the struggle to understand and let it slip from his mind, joining all the other things that don't make sense in this world.

'Ben, Ben. Want to climb on the cushion?' Ben looks at Alison from the corner of his eye, then reaches for my hand and pulls me with him towards a large air-cushion in the corner of Alison's playroom.

'That's it, Mum can come too,' says Alison.

Ben lets go of my hand and climbs onto the cushion. 'Up,' says Alison. It wobbles and he falls back onto the mattress. 'And down,' says Alison. After a few seconds, Ben laughs.

'Again?' he says.

'You want to get up and down again?' asks Alison, and he does, not just once but lots of times, laughing out loud as he falls. Alison starts rolling a fitness ball on top of his body when he is lying on the mattress and he loves that too.

After that, Ben rides on my back, crawls through a lycra tunnel, climbs into the ball pit, falls off more cushions and then sits on a square platform that swings from a hook in the ceiling. Alison pushes the platform back and forth gently as Ben and I pull fun faces at each other. He's been interacting with me or Alison for twenty minutes now, surely a record. And he likes the swinging platform. It's at this point that I start listening seriously to Alison, borrowing her books and entering the world of sensory integration therapy.

We establish what Alison calls Ben's sensory profile and Alison gives me a home program to work on between our visits to her. This covers Ben's desire for deep pressure, his balance, movement and body-position needs, improving his visual scanning and reducing his touch and hearing sensitivities. We also work on his fine motor skills and the ability to plan an action and then execute it. Very soon I start to notice that after Ben has done some weight-bearing activities, like trampolining or hanging from his hands or carrying something heavy, he becomes calmer and more ready to interact with me. This is what I most crave – the chance to play with my son, for him to have fun with me, not just look at me blankly and wander away.

The day we arrived in Perth – 14 April 1973, my mother tells me – was a perfect autumn day. My mother's friend drove us to the Mount Hotel, which sat at the base of Kings Park, between the city and the river. We stayed there for a few weeks while my mother house-hunted. It was only Pauline, Olivia and me with my mother; the older children and my father were in England until the end of the academic year. It felt warm that day. As we drove to the hotel, I saw a cloudless azure sky, the sort we rarely saw in England, and a silver-glinting river, wound around the city, curled between bridges and roads. Even through the car window, it was all clean and bright and shiny, as if this really was a new world. Everything looked different. The trees were sharp-edged, their leaves tinted with blue or grey and hanging from the branches in a loose, flickering way. It was supposed to be autumn, but most of the trees had leaves on them. I saw only one row of deciduous trees by the river; they were London plane trees, I think, but still, they looked strange with the high white light gleaming on their trunks.

The Mount Hotel had a small open-air swimming pool out the back and we decided we wanted to swim, even though it was unheated. Our friend laughed at us and said we'd be out like jacks-in-a-box. We weren't. The water was very cold but the sun felt warm on our backs and the air was as balmy as an English summer. Later that week, we saw a goat drinking from the pool. Well, that's what I remember, anyhow, although it seems unlikely.

It wasn't long before my mother found a house she liked. She rang my father and described it to him and he told her to go ahead and buy it. That autumn we sat on buffalo grass in the back garden, under the jacaranda and lilly-pilly trees and the endless sky, eating our lunches of bacon and egg sandwiches. My mother would point out the different plants and birds, trying to educate us. But it was the smells that amazed me most. Perth had a completely different palate of smells from anywhere else I'd been. You could walk along a street and suddenly smell honey or a dark peppery smell or spearmint or the scent of slightly overripe fruit. In the early morning when the magpies woke me, there was a smell of lemon, eucalyptus and hope. By lunchtime, the air was heavier and darker, smelling of warm grass and crushed ants. In the late afternoon a slightly tangy breeze came in, a fresh smell heralding the night-time scent of soap from our evening baths and fresh possum urine on the ceiling of our bedroom.

That year, the year I turned ten, seems like the beginning of my sensate self. It's as though the years before were dominated only by a fear of the senses and once we came to Australia, this changed. The shock of the new opened my senses and I started to notice the world. It continued to confound and frighten me at times, but much less so. Sensual pleasures became apparent to me. That first drive from the airport through a shining city and towards immersion in a swimming pool right on the edge of Kings Park shook me awake and kept me that way.

Even now, the most common landscape for my dreams is that stretch of road by the Swan River below Kings Park, a never-ending space of light that unfurls from the site of the Mount Hotel and ends at the house in Nedlands where we lived.

I'm determined to work on helping Ben to handle messy things. They regularly use paint or playdough at school and it will be a lot easier for him if he can enjoy the experience, or at least not freak out. I decide to try making soap. It's easy: all you need to do is mix soap flakes, water and essential oils and then mould the result into soap-shaped bars. I'm hoping the final products will make good gifts.

Actually, I don't like getting my hands messy either, but I feel I need to rise above this. We start with lavender – a nice safe smell. Ben does quite well. He squeezes the soap mixture in both hands until bits shoot out between his fingers like flying worms, then he rushes to the sink and washes his hands, wipes them dry on his clothes and has another squeeze.

'Make a shape, make a shape,' I keep saying, desperately trying to keep flecks of greyish looking slime out of my eyes.

'Make a shape, make a shape,' chants Ben as he squeezes and flicks soapy lavender mixture all over the kitchen. The doorbell rings and he rushes off to the door, soap in hand.

'Not in the lounge room, don't touch anything,' I shout, worried about the furniture but also slightly panicked from the squishy feeling on my hands.

'Stop, Ben, I need your hands,' I call, grabbing a towel and chasing him to the door. Two young men in suits and ties holding copies of the *Watchtower* stare at me apprehensively – am I mad or just doomed?

Later that day, we do eye exercises.

'Watch the little bear, Ben. No, keep your head still.'

He can't. I try to hold his head steady with one hand and move the bear with the other, but he still turns. I need three hands for this. Then I hold the little bear biscuit and he has to grab it with one hand as I move it across his mid-line.

'You have to sit still, Ben, and just grab with one hand.'

'I'll eat it now,' he says after he's got it. I only do four of these a night – I'm worried about his teeth, eating all those biscuits! Then we do catch and throw with a ball, not with much success, followed by a special hide and seek, where I place small chocolate buttons around the room and he has to find them. This encourages scanning and foreground-versus-background discrimination. After the eye exercises, Ben listens to three tracks of his therapeutic listening tape, purchased at great expense from the US. He quite likes this as it is electronically modified Mozart and Vivaldi. The idea is that it encourages Ben to focus on certain frequencies (like that of the human voice), become less defensive of other sounds and feel calm.

During the day I have also made Ben play at the park, jump on the trampoline, kick a soccer ball, try using pincher chopsticks to eat lunch, find tiny plastic animals in a tub of raw rice and beans and do funny animal walks. The only bits of this he actually enjoyed were the walks to and from the park (because he likes to read the numbers on the letterboxes), eating the treats, and me chasing him around the house with a towel.

I must admit to feeling dubious about the therapeutic listening. The information that I've read about this doesn't seem especially convincing, although, as usual, there are plenty of anecdotal comments from parents about its wondrous effect on their children. I'm slightly uneasy because it feels closer to reprogramming Ben's brain waves than the other forms of sensory integration therapy do. Of course I want him to be able to enjoy, not fear, sensations and to be able to do things that rely on good sensory integration, like riding a bike, using scissors and doing up buttons. But I can't help wondering if there might be some value in his sensory differences. When I express these doubts to Alison, she is polite and professional, though I can tell she thinks I'm misguided and a bit crazy. But I have been reading Diane Ackerman's book *A Natural History of the Senses*. I'm drawn to her comment:

> Deep down, we know our devotion to reality is just a marriage of convenience, and we leave it to the seers, the shamans, the ascetics, the religious teachers, the artists among us to reach a higher state of awareness, from which they transcend our rigorous but routinely analysing senses and become closer to the raw experience of nature that pours into the unconscious, the world of dreams, the source of myth.

What if some of Ben's 'dysfunction' is that raw experience? When we retrain his brain to process sensations the way we think is appropriate, the way that lets us live regular everyday lives in the Western world, do we also remove from him some vital source of dream and myth?

If, as Constance Classen argues, our understanding and classification of sensory experiences are culturally determined, then we could learn something from people who are outside the dominant culture. In the nineteenth and early twentieth centuries in particular, a number of famous 'wild' children were studied to determine which aspects of the senses were 'natural' and which culturally developed. The 'Wolf Children of India', the 'Wild Boy of Aveyron' and other 'wild' children all seemed to have extraordinarily strong senses of smell, very powerful but selective hearing and unusual visual processing – for example, difficulty distinguishing flat from three-dimensional sights and an inability to see landscape as anything other than a blur of colour and form. Classen suggests that smell is 'by nature of great importance to humans' and that it loses its importance only when suppressed by culture. She says: 'More than any other sense, smell seems to function as an indicator of presence and identity.'

Ben's sense of smell is always reliable. The other day Ben and Joe had been playing with identical toy rabbits – they'd received them from the local bread shop as part of some promotion. Laura reminded Joe to collect his bunny before they left, but he didn't know which of the two was his.

'Well, if they're the same, it doesn't matter,' said Laura.

'No! They are not the same. I want mine,' proclaimed Joe.

'Which is yours?' I asked Ben, knowing that he often notices small details that other people miss. Ben sniffed both toys and gave one to Joe, saying, 'That's yours.' Joe accepted this decision straightaway. Laura looked surprised and asked if she could smell them both.

'I can't tell any difference,' she commented to me quietly. 'Do you think Ben just did that to please Joe?'

'Oh no, he'll have recognised the different smells,' I said.

'But don't you think that's amazing?' asked Laura. I could see she was astonished so I said, 'I guess so.' But really, I didn't find it at all surprising. Every day after school when I give Ben a hug, I can tell by the scent of his hair which of his two education assistants has been with him that day. It's not that I actively smell him; it's just something that I notice.

Perhaps one day Ben could get a job in wine making, tea tasting or perfumery, all industries that rely on olfactory acuteness.

Did all the sensory integration therapy work? I'm not sure. I didn't notice any changes from the therapeutic listening, so we stopped after a couple of months. But the physical activities to work on Ben's vestibular and proprioceptive senses did seem to make a difference. He became less easily agitated and his motor skills improved. Over time, his sensitivity to noise and touch has lessened. He still dislikes loud noises but ordinary noises – like the everyday classroom noise of twenty-five children talking and working – are less of a problem now. His visual skills are improving and he can find words in a word-find puzzle more quickly than I can sometimes. He still rocks in his hammock and paces around rooms much of the day. I think he needs that motion.

Oliver Sacks argues that our body image is created through a combination of vision and our vestibular and proprioceptive systems. When any of these is faulty, not only do we not know where we are, but we also don't know who we are. I'm sure that Ben, in his early years, was without a sense of being in his own body. I think that he has now found his body-sense and has a feeling of continuity with his own past experiences.

Perhaps Ben would have developed in this way even without the sensory integration therapy. It's hard to tell. But for me, one of the greatest benefits of our weekly visits to Alison and the reading on sensory integration she gave me was the change in my view of myself. When I trampolined with Ben, I started to feel dizzy and ill long before he did. When we played with messy things, I looked around anxiously for a cloth to wipe my hands. I laughed with Alison about this.

'It's quite common for parents of the children I work with to be sensitive as well,' she explained.

When Ben felt overwhelmed after a day at school, I was reminded of myself at a shopping centre. I realised that I, too, had experienced sensory overload as a child and still do as an adult. Suddenly, moments of my past fell into place in a new way.

And I saw that Ben and I were alike in this way. It was like being given a wonderful gift. For several years, everything I had learnt about Ben had made him seem more distant from me. But now I could see the similarities between us. Instead of feeling puzzled and confused all the time, I started to understand some of his challenges. They weren't that different from mine, just magnified and more complex. I had rediscovered the sense of knowing my son from the inside out.

When I said that sensual pleasure began for me at age ten, of course I knew that couldn't be right. The senses are how we filter experience. We don't live without them or without the ability to feel sensory delight. Any pleasure I felt at ten must have been foreshadowed by earlier, similar experiences. I realise this, but still, it feels as though I only noticed the physical world and my bodily self when we came to Australia.

And then, in my early forties, I had another moment of awakening. I was in Melbourne for several days in the autumn and I walked around the parks, enjoying the feeling of a European autumn, the sort we don't get in Perth. The rest of the time I spent with M in a hotel room, falling into that hypnotic state of pleasure that sometimes happens between occasional lovers who are also good friends. The final night, M left me at midnight, looking for a moment like a little boy cast out of the toy room. But I was still in the room, that oasis of pleasure, and I felt as though M was there with me, that our conversation continued. I walked around the room naked, packing my bag, and I saw myself in the full-length mirror. It seemed to me that what I saw was not me – mother, daughter, wage-earner, soon to be ex-wife – but the pale fleshy woman of a Bonnard painting. I saw a woman just out of the bath perhaps – no longer young, but feminine, desirable.

The next morning, I woke early and had time to walk in the park near the hotel before I caught a taxi to the airport. I stepped into the crisp cold air of forty years ago. The exactness of cold on my face, letting me sense that I had hairs on my cheeks and that they quivered with the morning scents. The colour of my own breath as I breathed, slowly, slowly, into consciousness. The minutiae of my physical self coming from deep inside to greet me.

The oblique morning sun shunted through poplar leaves, glinting on the final drops of dew. I walked down the footpath, feeling the catch of coldness as I breathed, putting my hands up opposing sleeves because I had no pockets or gloves. Yellow poplars gave way to the sunset hues of plane trees, the red of liquidambars, brown oak leaves, silver birch trunks illuminated against the grass of the park. A small bough with red berries swung against my elbow. Acorns and leaves were squashed into the damp ground by my feet. A cacophony of inchoate memories tugged at me and I stopped, staring at autumn as if to drink it in, taking deep breaths, to hold it, to keep the smells, the images, the sounds. Never to lose this moment: the return of the sensuous body.

It seems that the body has its own memories, folded into secret spaces and coursing through the bloodstream. It remembers both pleasure and pain, both intimacy and distance. My body remembered the pleasures of an English autumn and, being cherished once more, gifted those pleasures back to me, forty years later. I realise now that my first ten years did include many positive sensory experiences but they were lost to my conscious mind when we left the place of my childhood. Perhaps the loss of all I had known didn't allow me to carry them with me to Australia.

*

'Mum, I need you,' calls Ben from the bedroom. I go in there and sit on his bed.

'Yes, Benji. Did you want something?'

'I made a space for you,' he says, lifting the sheet. I lie down beside him and he tucks his head under my chin. He feels warm and heavy the way children do just before they go to sleep. After a little while, I sit up and kiss him goodnight.

'You smell of lemon,' he says.

'Oh yes,' I say, 'I just finished a gin and tonic with a slice of lemon. Night, darling.'

'Goodnight,' he murmurs.

There's something very touching about the way Ben notices that I smell of lemon. It feels like an act of witnessing, an intimacy that only love allows. I wonder if years from now he will remember moments like this when a lemon-scented mother kissed him goodnight.

THE BLANK FACE

The awful thing is that beauty is mysterious as well as terrible.
—FYODOR DOSTOYEVSKY

'HOW DO I FEEL?'

Ben turns down the corners of his mouth and then checks the shape with his hands. His eyes thin a little and his forehead creases very slightly.

'Um, let me see now. Do you feel puzzled? Or worried?' I guess.

He shakes his head and asks again, 'How do I feel?'

'Maybe sad?'

'Why do I feel sad?' he asks, looking cheerful now that I've guessed his face correctly.

'I don't know, darling. Why are you sad?'

'You tell.'

'Well, you have to tell me, actually, because you're the sad one,' I explain.

'I don't know.'

'Oh, you feel sad but you don't know why. Is that it, Ben?'

'Yes.'

'Oh darling, come and have a cuddle.'

'No, thank you,' says Ben politely. He goes into my bedroom and stands in front of the mirror to practise his 'sad' face.

Ben finds it difficult to work out from body language, gesture and facial expressions how other people feel. Making eye
contact seems to be unhelpful in interpreting others and he
will often avoid it, though he doesn't seem to find it painful as
some autistic people do. He also has trouble accessing his own
feelings – not just identifying or naming his emotions, but even
recognising his biological and physiological states. By practis-
ing in front of the mirror, he may be trying to clarify his own
feelings. I watch him surreptitiously as he hams it up. I'm so
happy to see his face expressive.

When Ben was four years old, I was managing a work project
that involved travel interstate. I got my colleagues to do most
of the travelling, but eventually it became clear that I should
really go to Sydney, Canberra and Brisbane myself. After much
discussion with Robert, we agreed that I would go. I worried
about Ben; I'd never left him for more than twenty-four hours
before. I flew out on Tuesday morning and was back home by
midnight on Friday. Ben, of course, was asleep when I arrived.
The next morning when he woke, Robert got up and told him
that I was home in bed and that he could run in and say hello. I
knew Ben had missed me, and I was sure he would be excited
and happy to have me home. I sat up in bed, arms open for a
hug, as he walked into the room. He gave me a blank look and
then walked into the lounge. I got up and followed him.

'Aren't you going to say hello?' I asked.

'Hello,' he said, not looking up.

'Don't I get a hug?'

'I'm reading now.'

'Oh, yes, I see, okay.'

But it wasn't okay for me and I stood in the shower crying.
As I was dressing, I heard Robert talking to Ben, explaining to

him that I was sad he hadn't greeted me properly and that he should give me a hug. Then Ben came in and gave me a hug, before asking, 'What are we doing today?'

The episode has stuck in my mind because it was the moment when I first felt the full force of the blank autistic look. We got lots of blank looks from Ben, starting about age two and continuing for several years. He didn't look like that because he was angry that I had been away or as a punishment; it was just part of his repertoire at that time. Probably it struck me more this time because I'd been away and missing Ben and worrying about him missing me. The moment became emblematic. For months, I relived and grieved for that single moment when Ben walked into the bedroom and looked at me without interest or connection. Robert and I never spoke directly about it – he didn't want to reinforce my hurt, I suppose – but I did tell Penny about it. She sat opposite me, nodding occasionally as psychologists do, and her eyes filled with tears that never fell.

'I never thought I'd see that blank look again,' I said at one point. Only later did I realise the implications of this comment – the suggestion that a blank face from a loved one is something I remembered from a long time ago.

I am thinking that autism is to disability what cancer is to illness. I mean that autism now has a special status – a kind of 'oh no' status just like cancer. The word strikes fear into people just as the word cancer does. Like talking about the Big C instead of cancer, some people refer to autism as 'the A word', as in 'Don't say the A word to the mother, she'll freak out.'

In the way that people with cancer are told to 'fight' the disease, so too are parents of autistic children told to 'fight' autism, to rid the body and self of the autism that afflicts the child. I wonder if the parent of a child with Down syndrome or cerebral palsy would be told to work hard to eradicate the condition from their child? Or would they be expected to accept the condition and work hard instead to help their child fulfil his or her potential with the life they have been given?

Although cancer is not contagious, many people are afraid to be near someone with cancer. It is too close to death, perhaps. What is it that makes people afraid of contact with a person with autism? Difference, embarrassment, confusion? I wonder if there is something else there as well with autism, some deep recognition of the nature of the difference – that the soul of someone with autism may be a shape we don't recognise? Perhaps there is a kind of stain of shame that attaches itself to someone with autism, like someone with cancer, a shame connected to the feeling of incurability, their supposed proximity to non-being.

'Mum,' asked Ben, 'what's the opposite of normal?' I was about to say abnormal without thinking, when he supplied his own answer: 'Special.'

'Is that what the teacher at school says?' I asked.

'I'm not saying,' he replied.

Some parents I know won't describe their child as autistic in spite of a medical diagnosis. They argue that the word autism is limiting and stigmatising. They will often refuse to use the term disability or disabled as well. They may talk about their 'child with special needs' or even their 'special child'. I feel uncomfortable about this. I want to be able to say that Ben is autistic and to remove the stigma from autism. Talking about 'special needs' can be a double-edged sword: it suggests that all other children have the same 'normal' and therefore appropriate needs but that our child has needs that are inappropriate or should be considered a drain on the public purse. In many areas of life, typically developing children, too, have different needs from one another. As people with disabilities have pointed out, if the world were structured differently (for example, if all technology were developed using universal design principles), then the needs of someone with a disability would not be 'special' at all.

When we call our child special, I think we should mean that they are special to us as all children are, as those we love are special. I don't want to say Ben is special because of his neurological make-up. Nor do I want to idealise my son. Kamran Nazeer, an autistic writer, says: 'When we call someone a genius, or special, or extraordinary, we mean that they are blessed with a natural faculty that we are not. They are different from us. We cannot understand them.' This, he believes, helps us feel safe; we remove from ourselves the need to engage with someone we have labelled 'special'.

The popularity of the 'special' word reminds me of the many times I have read the comment that children with autism are typically very beautiful, like angels. In my experience, most young children are attractive. I don't believe that autistic children are any more or less physically attractive than others. But there are theories about the beauty of autistic children (though none about autistic adults, as far as I know). Doreen Virtue, author of *The Care and Feeding of Indigo Children*, claims they are special 'Indigo' children, sent 'to mash down old systems that no longer serve us'. Although sometimes she thinks they are misdiagnosed and are in fact a new breed of 'Crystal' children: 'The first thing most people notice about them ... is their eyes, large, penetrating and wise beyond their years.' They are not fully of this world, God's little angel messengers. Others have argued that perhaps autistic children are considered beautiful because they are always staring intently and solemnly, thus creating attractive images in photos. Another theory is that autism may be caused partly by antibiotics given for ear infections, that children with small heads and narrow ear passages are more likely to get ear infections, and that we typically find smaller, more symmetrical faces attractive. Nazeer connects the notion of beauty in autistic children to our protective instincts: 'Other people want to protect them, to care for them; it is remarkable, for example, how often even clinicians mention that autistic children have beautiful eyes.' To me, all this physical beauty stuff is just a way of saying we construct autism as 'other' and therefore valorise and stigmatise, idealise and demonise.

The funny thing about me rejecting the 'beautiful angel' theory of autism is that Ben truly is a beautiful boy, and one who looks nothing like either of his parents! Of course, all parents think their own children are beautiful, but many other people have commented on Ben's good looks. Because his skin is so fair, I keep him smothered with sun lotion and make him wear a hat and as a result his face is still creamy, with only four or five freckles. This and his blue eyes and pale straw hair may make him look less worldly and masculine than other boys his age. And he has small, neat features, as in the stereotype. Unlike the stereotype, however, Ben laughs a lot and photographs never seem to show him solemn, preoccupied or focused, even though he can be all of these things at times. I surprise myself by finding him most beautiful when he eats – he seems both avid and innocent in a way that touches me deeply.

'You're lucky he's so good looking,' said a friend. 'People will be much nicer to him because of that. They'll make more allowances at school.'

'Maybe people will be nice because they like him,' I replied.

'Oh yes, of course!'

Beauty as God's consolation prize.

*

There is a boy with sad almond eyes who still haunts me. He lay on the floor at the 'special needs' playgroup and held two plastic trucks by his face, watching them, moving them only slightly. He appeared oblivious to everyone and everything else in the room. I sat down with him and talked to him gently, saying 'Hello' and 'Nice trucks'. Then I moved one of the trucks away a bit and then towards him several times, saying, 'You want the truck.' For a little while there was no reaction, then he sat up and became upset. He tried to lock the two trucks together, getting agitated. I reached to help him, but he didn't want me there and he cried. His face became creased, his eyes turned down like half-moons, a strange small sound came out of his mouth and he turned his head to find his mum.

'It's okay,' I said to him, 'it's okay,' and backed away. He stopped his sad noises and lay back down, face towards the trucks, hand on top of them. He looked about four years old and yet his emotional competence seemed that of a six-month-old baby. It was his face that got me – such terribly confused and sad eyes in a face trying to blank out all other sensations.

There are so many of them, these sad little boys (mostly boys, only occasionally girls) whose biological challenges mean they can't embrace the world and its people. Everything that can make childhood wonderful for other children seems to pain these boys.

Ben was never like that. He always had some connection to the outside world and its people. It was tenuous at times, but we could always reach him. His sense of humour saved him – and me perhaps – because it enabled us to tease and laugh with him, to show him we loved him and would make the world safe for him.

Well, we couldn't, we can't, make the world safe, but it has gradually become safer for him to step out of self-containment and into connection.

The almond-eyed boy I can't forget was just one of six boys at the playgroup. I went along as an 'expert' parent volunteer, that is, someone who'd had a disabled child for a while and therefore 'knew the ropes'. My role was to chat to the parents and then, when they went into an information session, to help look after the children. As it happened, when the presentation started, the one-year-old sibling of the almond-eyed boy was grizzling and needed to be rocked off to sleep, so I got to cuddle him instead. He cried for a few minutes and I noticed that his older brother looked up with an agonised face, but then the baby dropped off to sleep and I sat with him on my shoulder, watching the others. The boy with almond eyes lay on the floor in a posture we would normally describe as despairing. No one interrupted him. Then it was time for me to pick Ben up from school. I was glad to leave, glad to get into the sunshine, very glad to see Ben come out of class towards me in all his self-ness.

Later, though, that boy kept coming into my mind. His strangely stiff but hurt face when his mum went into the other room for the presentation. His still body as he lay on the wooden floor. His eyes – almost completely vacant except for those shafts of sadness and panic.

Later still I realised that what I felt was fear. It ran through me, past my chest, rising occasionally into my throat and then settling for a time in my gut. I don't know if it was fear for him, and boys like him (that's what I wanted it to be), or fear for Ben, or my own childhood fear of the world revisiting me, or some sort of primitive fear of these children as 'the other'.

Why do we fear the strangeness of others so much?

A few years ago, Ben and I were in the Tropicana Café in Fremantle. I drank a café latte and read the newspaper. Ben ate a muffin and recited the text of his favourite book, *Cat Balloon*. He wandered around the café between bites, moving past people as if they were furniture, talking all the while, laughing quite often.

'Hello, what is your name?' asked a young man with dishevelled hair, scruffy clothes and a backpack.

Ben ignored him. *'Cat balloon did not hear their loud cries, he and the moon danced away through the sky.'*

The young man followed Ben and tried several times to engage him. Ben brushed him off as if he were a fly. The man then did a handstand and made funny sounds (the Tropicana is a café where you can do such things). He still couldn't get Ben's attention, so he reached out to grab Ben's shoulders, to make him pay attention. Within seconds, Ben had retreated to my side and I had half-risen in my chair and placed my arms around him. I felt the desperation in the young man and everything in me wanted to push him away, place a barrier between him and Ben. I wanted to do this because I felt the man was disturbed in some fundamental way.

The young man put out his hand to shake mine and say hello.

'What is his name?' he asked.

'His name is Ben.'

'Hey! Hello, Ben, my name too is Benjamin.' He had a Germanic-sounding accent.

'I'm Rachel,' I said. 'Where are you from?'

'The universe,' he answered.

'I wondered if your accent was German.'

'Ben, look!' A cartwheel. Ben glanced at him and then moved off to eat some muffin and wandered over to the other side of the café. German Ben followed him, trying to get Ben to play with him. He spoke some German to him – at least I assumed it was German. Ben continued to treat him like a bothersome object, but German Ben was insistent. He wanted very much to get a response.

Eventually I said to him, 'He's in a world of his own. He's like that sometimes.' I was getting a little annoyed with this man who was interrupting my coffee and Ben's pleasure. I wondered if his name really was Benjamin.

'No, no, you must not let him. I know what it is. Ben, you must talk to me,' he said, grabbing Ben's arm again. 'I understand, I was brought up in a Home, I understand.' He was passionate by then, quite distressed because Ben was not relating to him. I moved to stand between the two of them. I could see that my Ben was finally paying enough attention to this other adult to indicate that he was slightly troubled by him.

'It's okay,' I said, though which Ben I was speaking to I'm not sure. 'We're ready to go now. Ben, put on your hat,' I said to my Ben. He heard that and actually went to the table and put on his hat, sideways, so the neck flap was half over his eyes. German Ben tried to stop us, still quite vehement that he knew what was happening and that he could help. In the end I had to be almost rude to get out of the café and even then he followed us, talking to Ben, desperately trying to get something back. I turned and said, 'Please just leave him alone now. Goodbye,' picked Ben up and walked across the road.

What I think now is: how clear it is to a so-called 'normal' person (I still think of myself that way) when someone is different in some fundamental way, like German Ben – due to a psychiatric illness, I'd guess – or like my Ben, due to a neurological condition. And how easily the German man recognised Ben's non-responsiveness as dangerous, how much he wanted to connect with him.

Faced with the German, I felt compassion, admiration and fear in about equal measures. And I had a sense that Ben knew that this man was not a safe or fun person to be with, in spite of the cartwheels. How did he know that? Was it coming from me or did he pick up the desperate edge?

That poor young man saw in Ben his own childhood self, damaged perhaps through neglect or abandonment or lack of mothering. He didn't want another child to go through what he had. I notice that he didn't know or care that he was invading Ben's space, and mine. He wanted to save Ben, I suppose.

Everyone wants to rescue Ben.

To rescue or to deny – that seems to be our reaction to certain types of disability. What the writer Thomas Couser describes as the 'cure or kill' approach.

Does Ben ever feel shame because he is different or disabled? I don't know, but I don't think he does (yet). In her book about shame, Elspeth Probyn suggests that shame only operates after interest or enjoyment has been activated and when we care about the interest of others. So perhaps Ben isn't connected enough with others to feel shame. Perhaps he doesn't care enough about others' interest in him. Probyn suggests that shame arises as a primal reaction to the possibility of love – both loving and being loved – and love's possible incompleteness. While it is clear that Ben experiences love, perhaps he doesn't experience the fear of its loss. Or perhaps he does feel shame but doesn't express it in the ways we might recognise, like blushing, squirming, expressing a sense of unease and self-consciousness in front of another.

Probyn quotes Gerhardt Piers: 'Behind the feeling of shame stands not the fear of hatred, but the fear of contempt which, on an even deeper level of the unconscious, spells fear of abandonment ... death by emotional starvation.' This may give us a hint as to why some parents of autistic children feel shame associated with their child's diagnosis. We expect uncon-ditional love from our young children – it can feel shameful that your child doesn't love you in quite the way you want or expect. It may be the most important relationship of your life and you may love your child completely and unconditionally, but there is always a kind of space between him and you, a taste of the emotional starvation we all fear deeply.

I am walking downstairs in a white nightdress and no shoes. The carpet is an evil orange and black pattern. At the edge of each step are rough wooden boards covered in dust. At the bottom of the stairs I turn right. Cold air brushes the hair on my arms. When I reach the door, I pause, and for a moment I am about to go back upstairs. But I don't. The door is ajar and I look through the crack. She sits at the table, her back to the door, the desk lamp creating a cone of light around her head. I can see her reflection in the window across the room. She is writing, hunched over her paper, head down, lips moving. I push the door open. She hears me and moves, her reflected face smudging. She turns and a skeleton face is before me – a blank skull with white bones and stones for eyes. No, not stones – mother of pearl, its clouded milk sheen glinting in the lamplight.

It's dark. I glance at the clock – 6 a.m. Beside me, Robert is lying on his back and doing his quiet morning snores. Ben is silent, but he will wake soon. I feel chilled from the dream about my mother's face and don't want to sleep again, so I get out of bed quietly, pull on my tracksuit and slippers and close the bedroom door behind me. I fill up the kettle, reach for a mug and tea bag. The feeling of the dream lingers. The orange and black carpet, jagged in my memory, the cold air rushing through the house, how the front door rattled on windy days. And the memory of the doorway into my mother's study, how I often paused there, wondering if I should interrupt her after all.

My mother sat in a circle of light, writing and thinking, thinking and writing, not words, but strange symbols and numbers she called her work. As a child I knew how important that work was. You could see it was important by the way she never wanted to leave it, by the way she and my father discussed it at nights, he walking up and down in front of the empty grate, she sitting in her chair by the lamp, twisting her right hand around the left shoulder of her jumper or blouse, fiddling with the material. You could see it was special work, too, when you looked at it, because only my parents could read it. The mystery of it was its own eloquence, its own drama. I knew I shouldn't interrupt her, but I couldn't always prevent myself from doing so.

I could interpret my dream this morning as a reminder of my mother's seeming inaccessibility, of her focus on her work. But there is another possible reading. Perhaps the woman in the study, the woman with the bone face and mother of pearl eyes, is actually me.

Daniela Dawes is well groomed, dressed in brown and sits neatly in her chair, with very little movement. Her daughter sits beside her, a lock of blonde hair lying over one eye. Dawes stops to think before she answers a question and then talks clearly and deliberately, without showing any emotion. The only sign that she has been through trauma, that this conversation might be traumatic for her, is the way she uses the date itself – August 4 – to stand in for the act that she performed that day, the day she killed her son.

'I had a few major things, tragic things, happen in a very short period of time, so what happened on August 4 was really about depression, in that I was overwhelmed by what was happening in my life and I was having feelings of not being able, not wanting to be here anymore ... And I had always known ... that Jason would have to be with me. That is how August 4 happened.'

Jenny Brockie, the interviewer, asks, 'Do you feel, in any way, that it [killing Jason] was justified?'

'No, never. You cannot justify that.' Still no sign of emotion.

I am watching a video of SBS's *Insight* program called 'Understanding Autism', which aired in late 2006. Although the interview with Dawes and her daughter runs for only eight minutes and is completely devoid of overt expressions of emotion, it is the defining segment of the program. We are watching a woman who killed her autistic ten-year-old and then tried to kill herself. We are also watching her sixteen-year-old daughter – the child she didn't kill.

'And how did you feel about what happened?' Brockie asks the daughter.

The daughter tips her head slightly towards Brockie and says, 'The way I coped with it was by blocking out all emotion to it and I guess, in a way, I did not really, I have not really dealt with it because I don't really have emotion about it because it is too difficult to put emotion into it.'

Daughter, like mother, is composed; it is the tightly held and frightening composure of someone who has had to face the incomprehensible. To watch them is both heart-rending and shocking, all the more so because of their lack of expression.

It is a relief when Brockie turns and asks questions of other audience members. She asks a woman with an autistic son how she feels listening to this story. This woman seems close to breakdown. She cries as she says that she thinks about her son dying almost every day, that the demands of caring for her son are destroying her family, and that she can't get any real help. The camera pans to other faces, all shown in close-up. Some are nodding in understanding or agreement, some look concerned, some are blank. Once again, I think about the role of the blank face in autism – how painful it is when your child's face is blank to you, how in self-protection you may end up blanking your face to your child.

This program is just one example of recent media coverage of autism. A number of common threads run through this coverage: the increased numbers of children diagnosed, the controversies over cause and treatment, the lack of funding for timely and appropriate intervention, the lack of support for families, and the stress and distress that having an autistic child places on families, particularly mothers. Underlying this last point is, I think, an unspoken assumption that it is a tragedy to have a child with autism.

Brockie asks a mother of three autistic children whether, if she had known in advance that she would have this experience of parenting, she would still have had children.

'I would probably have held back and not had children,' she replies.

Although at some level I understand the despair this mother must be feeling, still it is painful to hear her response. I know that for me, it would be a tragedy to lose Ben, a tragedy never to have known him. But I also know that every parent's experience is different and that the support available is just not enough for many families.

Of course, most parents adore their children, autistic or neurotypical, but it is surely partly the message that autistic children are a burden to their parents that supports the search for a 'cure'. Groups like Cure Autism Now and Autism Speaks (both established by parents to raise money to explain the genesis of and find a 'cure' for autism) are often criticised by autistic people for wanting to prevent the birth of future autistic people. Aspies for Freedom, for example, say on their website: 'We know that autism is not a disease, and we oppose any attempts to "cure" someone of an autism spectrum condition, or any attempts to make them "normal" against their will.'

Why would you want to cure someone of being themselves?

'I am not a puzzle, I am a person.' These are the words on the badges distributed by the Autistic Liberation Front, a movement of individuals with autism whose goals include celebrating autism, stopping the search for a cure and defending the dignity of autistic citizens.

The slogan goes to the very core of the dilemma of parenting a child with autism. How many times have I said about Ben, 'I don't understand him,' or 'He's so different from me,' or 'His mind is a mystery'? And how many times have I seen the analogy of a puzzle used in the scientific search for an 'answer' to autism? Our state association even uses a jigsaw puzzle as its logo.

Ben *is* profoundly puzzling to me at times. I suspect I am puzzling for him. But then, I am puzzling to myself also. Having a child whose experience is so different from your own, who challenges all your ideas about 'normality' and reality, a child whose senses appear to work differently, whose brain is differently wired – having a child like this makes you question your own assumptions, your ideas about what is and who you are.

When I read the words 'I am not a puzzle, I am a person' and the goals of the Autistic Liberation Front, I felt like cheering out loud. I have always felt uncomfortable about the idea that Ben can be 'cured', 'recovered' or 'behaviourally modified'. I want him to be himself, whoever that is. But still, I do consider him a mystery. Seeking to interact with the unknown doesn't need to involve judgement. Difference doesn't need to imply hierarchy. Ben is a mystery to me at times, but so are other people. With Ben it's simply that the mystery is foregrounded – our usual assumptions of shared values and ways of thinking are demonstrated to be false and so we are thrown back on the unknowability of the other.

Some time ago we spent the night in a railway cottage in the bush. Ben happily explored the property, had a late dinner with us at the local tavern and then went to sleep in the single bed in the carriage. He woke at 5 a.m. and said, 'I don't know where I am, it's dark, I can't see.' I called out to him to go back to sleep, but he said several times, 'I don't know where I am,' so I got up and climbed into bed with him. He cuddled into me, his chin against my cheek, his knees poking into my tummy.

'I didn't know where I was,' he explained.

'Yes, I know, but I'm here now, it's okay,' I said.

And it was okay. He felt safe again. I am often moved by the enormous power of the mother's body. Just to lie beside him, holding him, was enough. These things feel miraculous to me. Is this so for every mother? I remember the way Ben used to cry and cry at night even when I was with him, patting him, holding him. I would breastfeed him and then he would cry as soon as I put him down or as soon as he woke. Perhaps that makes his connection to me now seem extraordinarily precious, a gift that I feared I would never receive.

It is at times like this, when physical closeness is enough, that I feel again the merging of mother and child, the sense once more that Ben came from my body and is still of my body. His beauty and his mystery are not confounding, but simply present.

WINDING

We are brought out of darkness and error.—BOOK OF COMMON PRAYER

'DO YOU REMEMBER WHEN I was in kindy?'

'Yes, of course I do, Ben.'

'Before recess we had to read a number the teacher wrote on the board. All the other kids read one to nine. I was reading over one hundred. Remember that, Mum?'

'Yes, I remember.'

'I was unique not technique.'

'What's technique?'

'You know, Mum, if you're not unique.'

No one really knows what causes autism. In fact, researchers are no longer looking for one cause, but rather for a variety of causes that may result in a range of types of autism spectrum disorder. But all the different theories include the notion of error – a mistake of nature, environment or humankind. It could be a genetic mutation, a chemical imbalance, the introduction of toxins or an incident during pregnancy or childbirth.

It's strange to feel that something fundamental about your child is due to error. Strange and uncomfortable. It can induce a sense of guilt – what did I do to cause this? Or it can result in bitter anger against the supposed cause of the condition, like parents who blame the measles, mumps and rubella vaccine. Or it can drive parents to fight back, to attempt to reverse the error through therapy or dietary regimes.

I have trouble accepting these views. I don't accept that anything about Ben is an error. It feels to me that he is the way he must be. The behaviours and ways of thinking that we group under the term autism seem fundamentally a part of his character, not a mistake to be removed or an imposition to be fought. I appreciate that I may see it this way because Ben is high-functioning: he can communicate, he copes with daily life quite well and he is of above-average intelligence. And of course, if I could wish away his disadvantages and struggles, I would. But I don't have an idea of who he would be if he didn't think and behave the way we label autistic. The child I once imagined I knew – the child I imagined Ben to be when he was a baby – has no currency now. I let that other Ben go a long time ago. I no longer think about or mourn him. The Ben I know and love is not the result of an error, an accident or toxicity – he is his true self, the person he is meant to be.

'There's no such thing as a true self, though, is there?' remarked Ben's paediatrician. 'We mould our children and we want to encourage Ben to be less autistic, more normal. Isn't that what you want?'

The *Oxford English Dictionary* offers six different groups of definitions for the noun 'error'. They include what one might expect: 'the holding of mistaken notions or beliefs' and 'something incorrectly done through ignorance or inadvertence'. There is also a definition that links error to wrongdoing: 'a departure from moral rectitude; a transgression'. New to me is the poetic use in English imitating the Latin meaning of error as 'the action of roaming or wandering; hence a devious or winding course, a roving, winding'.

I first imagined a girl child. I met J in my late twenties and we were lovers for three years. It was during this time that the little girl began to visit me, first at night in my dreams and then later during the day as well.

Her name was Alice. She seemed to be about four or five years old. She was thin, with pale skin and stick-like legs. Her hair was straight and cut short at the chin, just like mine had always been as a child, but Alice's hair was straw-coloured, not brown, and her eyes were clear blue, much bluer than my own. Like me, she was shy and quiet. When she appeared, she always stayed close to me, like a shadow. In my dreams, she spoke and laughed. In the daytime, she was silent.

We talked about having a child, J and I. We agreed we would, when his own children were older. Then he changed his mind; children were too much work, he said. After we stopped seeing each other, Alice appeared less often and mainly at night. She went underground.

Years later – about ten years later – I actually met a child who seemed to be just as I remembered, or imagined, Alice. She was the oldest daughter of a friend. I took four-year-old Ben around to visit them one day, and there was Alice, five years old and exactly as I had known she would be, not just physically but in her character, too. She stood at her mother's side and stared at Ben, her blue eyes wide, like a child in a picture book. Her three-year-old sister was similar to her, but less shy, more chatty. They showed me all their favourite toys, watched Ben with a funny mix of curiosity and concern, and retreated regularly to their mother's body. Ben counted the number of pickets in their fence and then walked in circles around a bike, repeating the text of a forty-minute video he had watched the night before. Then he said, 'You're ready to go home now,' (meaning he was ready) and we left. The girls looked confused and relieved at the same time.

Driving home in the car, Ben repeated the video text once more and I cried. (That was the year I was always crying in the car, because it seemed to be the only private place, and Ben didn't notice or care.) It was a shock seeing in the flesh a child so like the one who had visited me. I knew by then I would never have a daughter. And my son was so different from other children, our relationship so different from other parents' relationships with their children.

Bruno Bettelheim is famous – or perhaps infamous – for his erroneous theory on the origins of autism. In his 1967 book *The Empty Fortress*, Bettelheim elaborated on Leo Kanner's idea that autism in children may be related to parenting, an idea that Kanner himself later recanted. Bettelheim's book publicised the phrase 'refrigerator mother', claiming that autistic children's behaviour was retaliation against a cold, rejecting mother and an absent father. A survivor of Dachau and Buchenwald, Bettelheim compared the relationship between mother and autistic child to that of Nazi officer and camp prisoner. He also described the mothers of autistic children as 'devouring witches', recognised by children in fairytales like Hansel and Gretel. As the director of the residential Orthogenic School for disturbed children in Chicago, Bettelheim claimed to have cured many autistic children through his 'milieu therapy' approach.

According to Richard Pollack, Bettelheim's biographer, *The Empty Fortress* received significant coverage in the popular press, with laudatory reviews in *Scientific American*, the *New*

York Times, the *New Yorker* and *Time*. Bettelheim was interviewed on the *Today* show and other television and radio stations across America. A number of academic reviewers did question the book's theoretical rigour and cast doubt on Bettelheim's approach to autism, but these reviews were in the more academic journals and not accessible to the general public. For many years after the publication of this book, parents – in particular the 'refrigerator mothers' – were blamed for their children's autism and the most common treatment option offered was removal of the child into institutional care. Bettelheim was not the only psychologist or scientist in the 1960s who believed that autism was the result of poor parenting, but he was the man who popularised the theory. Even after the psychogenic approach to autism was discounted by most scientists and clinicians, *The Empty Fortress* was still one of the most common books on autism to be found in public libraries around the world.

It's not hard to see how a superficial study of mothers with their autistic children might result in a belief that the mothers are cold and withholding. If your child ignores you, or bites, hits and screams at you, you will tend to withdraw. Likewise, if your child fears eye contact, seems pained by physical touch and gets upset at the sound of spontaneous affection or lively conversation, you will moderate your behaviour and voice to keep your child calm. And of course, when you visit psychiatrists, psychologists and other professionals for help with your child, you are likely to be anxious, confused and depressed. So perhaps this type of behaviour encouraged the cold-mother theories. But more important, I think, is the fact that this all occurred in the post-war era, when women were being relegated to the home once more and when theories about the importance of the mother–child attachment were being popularised. It wasn't until the 1980s that the refrigerator mother theory was replaced by our current understanding that autism is caused by biological or neurological damage.

We first saw Ben when he was a seven-week-old foetus. It was January. I lay on the table and a doctor we'd never met before and never saw again gently moved the ultrasound wand over my stomach. He held it still, then pressed down slightly.

'See, see your baby?' We looked at a black and white image on a TV screen, saw smudgy grey things.

'See the heartbeat?' he asked. I couldn't.

'Don't worry,' he said, 'you will.' He waited while my eyes adjusted to the screen's confusion and I saw a tiny flicker. On, off, on, off.

'Is that it?'

'Yes, that's your baby's heartbeat.'

That was our initial glimpse of Ben, a foetus the size of a bean. Tears came into my eyes and Robert said, 'It's like seeing a star in another galaxy through a telescope.' The doctor smiled – he was used to giving gifts – and handed me a photo.

Then there was that single moment, opening infinite spaces. Years of hope, months of waiting, hours of struggle, and the moment of birth is so brief. In the mirror I saw the head crown and the midwife said, 'Stop pushing now.' But it was beyond my control and I could only watch the tearing as the head ripped through. A few seconds later a baby lay on my chest, still connected to me. I gazed at his small square face and wizened body. Laid one hand gently on his crinkled skin. In that moment, I knew him.

Even before I first breastfed Benjamin, I had fallen in love with him. He was completely recognisable to me. I felt I knew him as I knew the sound of my own breathing. For eighteen months, everything that followed seemed expected. I seemed to know how he would be and why.

That's what I remember feeling.

The notion of damage and error, of course, suggests an opposite – something whole, correct, perfect. However much we struggle against it, we can't seem to give up the notion of perfection. And nowhere is it more obvious than with a newborn baby. The first thing people say is, 'Isn't she perfect?' We know that babies and children are not perfect, but still we can't resist the awe that is inspired when we see a newborn, fresh in the world, naked and defenseless. The idea of perfection merges with innocence and purity, the lack of any moral or spiritual blemish.

In some cultures it is sacrilegious to aim for perfection in matters human-made. The perfect is the realm of the gods and humans must make do with imperfection. This is the idea behind the single flaw in a handmade Persian rug or the spirit line in a Guatemalan weaving. As well as recognising the difference between human and god, these flaws become the spaces through which the spirits may enter and leave.

It is reassuring, I think, that the spirits enter through the cracks.

It might seem strange, having wanted a daughter so much, that I was happy when I found out that our baby would be a boy. We were told halfway through the pregnancy. But in some way, I had been expecting a boy anyhow. I was so happy to be pregnant that the sex of the baby was not important to me. When we knew it was a boy I felt relief run through me – a boy, not a miniature Rachel after all, but someone new. Someone who would be able to develop all by himself, in his own way. I felt a boy wouldn't be at risk of being too much like me. I thought: I won't have to worry so much about being a good mother to a boy.

Out of nowhere comes a memory of when I was eight months pregnant. I park my car outside the government office where I am due for a meeting. It is a cold but sunny August morning. I am wearing black maternity trousers and a deep-red velvet maternity top. I don't need a jacket because the baby keeps me warm. The top is my favourite piece of maternity clothing. I don't know it now, but it will be the only item I keep after the baby is born. This should be one of my last work meetings – the baby is due in four weeks and I want to finish work two weeks before he arrives. I sail along the pavement, my belly huge in my wonderful red velvet. At least, I feel that I sail; really I know that I waddle like an overfed turkey. On the other side of the road is a park and I see a ragged line of silent people. They are homeless people, mostly men, and their stances are downbeat – they are tired or cold or hungry. Probably all three. There is no hope in their body language and seeing them like that strikes a chill through me. A small white van drives up and I realise that this is a mobile soup kitchen. My pace slows and my hand rests on my belly and a shot of fear runs through me: what if my son is one day one of these men?

I remember that moment now because it was unusual. Once I was pregnant and it was clear the baby was likely to develop to full maturity, I was relaxed and optimistic. I didn't worry about the baby being ill or disabled; I didn't worry about the birth; I didn't feel concerned about how my life would change with a new baby. During our fertility treatment I kept thinking: maybe I'm not meant to be a mother, maybe that's why I can't become pregnant. But once I was pregnant, those feelings disappeared. I wasn't unfit to be a mother: my body had finally proved that.

I have never and will never regret having my son, but sometimes I wonder if the attempt to have a child with medical assistance wasn't deeply selfish. Perhaps I was too old, or my genes somehow damaged, or the combination of genes not right. If I ignored an 'error' message from nature, I'm so glad I did.

There are many examples of errors resulting in new discoveries, particularly in the sciences, but also in other fields. A friend mentioned one that appeals to me. She told me that the original gâteau was actually a mistake. A French chef was making a cake and it failed and collapsed. He dressed it up with cream and fruit and chocolate shavings and thus created the sort of cake we call gâteau. I don't know if this is a true story or not – but I believe it anyhow.

He was such a quaint baby. He was thin and long with wrinkled skin and a white face. His hair was like pale straw and his eyes blue. He was all crescents – arched back, curly hair, turned-down mouth, half-moon eyelids, thumbs like baby semi-circles gesturing dizzily around his head. Even his feet seemed to form arcs, drawing me to run my tongue under his soles and then kiss his tiny toes.

Although he was long, Ben was a small baby and he was hungry. He fed – scrappily at first – every two or three hours. Once he had learned to open his mouth, latch on and suck properly (and this took six weeks), he would stare up at me with his sea-blue eyes, let his whole body relax into my arms and lay one hand on my breast, as if to hold me in place. This was the only time he seemed relaxed and at ease in the world or his body. The rest of the time he was restless.

As soon as I'd put him down or get him settled with one toy, he'd move or grizzle until I moved him. He wanted attention – to be held, mostly. He wouldn't sit in his pram and watch people pass. Sometimes he didn't even want to be taken out for a walk in the pram – he'd get uncomfortable or unhappy. We didn't know why or what he felt, just that he seemed to need constant distractions, constant holding. Loud noises startled him terribly and he would cry when someone sneezed or a crow cawed.

For his first four months he would only sleep if he was skin to skin with me or Robert. We sat in an old cream rocking chair in the lounge room and rocked him to sleep on our shoulders, patting him and rocking back and forth for an hour or more before he would sleep and then sitting still until he woke because if we put him down or moved he would wake and cry and cry. In the evening, I fed him to sleep and he spent the nights in our bed, lying between me and a homemade wooden rail to stop him falling to the floor.

When he was four months old, we moved him into the cot in his own bedroom next door. He woke every hour or two, every night for two years, and each time he woke, I got up and sat by his cot and patted and sang him back to sleep. I'd sit on a chair with my hand through the cot bars and my head resting on the top of the cot. Sometimes I would sleep before Ben did and I would wake an hour later, stiff and cold with a deep indentation across my forehead.

When Ben was about one, I remember a friend saying to me that it was a shame that he was such a 'demanding baby'. I hadn't thought of him as demanding and I didn't agree with her comment. I just recognised his need for closeness and reassurance. I suppose I thought all babies were like this, even though a basic observation of other babies should have shown me that this wasn't the case. I read his need for attention as part of his great interest in the world. Ben – when he was sitting – had a way of sitting straight and forward in his pram or on the floor. He seemed always alert. The hair at the back of his head was fluffy and messy whereas the top and sides were neat, so he was woolly as he sat, a characteristic 'just woken up and interested' look about him. He was always watching things – shafts of light, passing shadows, the moving branches of trees, objects seen through windows, things with bright colours and interesting shapes. The first time we went to the beach, he took a huge gulp of air and his whole face seemed to change with the shock of it. His eyes grew larger, his cheeks quivered and his forehead creased in amazement. He was only three months old. 'Look,' said Robert, 'he loves the sea air.'

Bruno Bettelheim, once famous for his miracle cures of autistic and psychotic children, his articles on behaviour in concentration camps and his book on fairytales, is now famous for his lies, his anti-Semitism, his plagiarism and his abuse of damaged children. Soon after his death by suicide in 1990, former residents and staff at the Orthogenic School began to talk publicly about Bettelheim's dictatorial style and the ill-treatment of residents. In 1997, Richard Pollack published his biography, *The Creation of Dr B.* This book tells a fascinating story of a complex, charismatic and highly intelligent man who fabricated his way through life. Bettelheim's deceptions stretched from his supposed qualifications in psychology in Austria before the war and the nature of his experiences in and release from Dachau and Buchenwald, to the scientific credibility of his work and his sources. Many of the 'autistic' children he 'cured' at the Orthogenic School were never diagnosed as autistic. Some of the children he claimed went on to normal adult life did not do so. Many of the anecdotes he used in his articles and books on the school were fabricated to make a point.

Pollack doesn't attempt to explain why Bettelheim told so many lies about his own life and his professional work. However, he suggests that the deceit started opportunistically when Bettelheim arrived in the USA in 1939 and applied for university posts for which he was unqualified. Once he was director at the Orthogenic School, his total control over all aspects of the school and lack of accountability to anyone enabled him to pursue his own ideas about child development. If his theories were not supported by the facts, he simply changed the facts, sure that his theory was right and that time would prove that to be the case. Clearly, Bettelheim was traumatised by the early death of his father from syphilis and from his ten months in concentration camps prior to the outbreak of the war. Pollack suggests that Bettelheim's hatred of mothers stemmed partly from his feeling that his own mother rejected him. Writing about Paul Celan's poem 'Todesfuge', in which there are references to the 'black milk' of the Nazi death camps, Bettelheim rejected the normal interpretation of black milk as the smoke from the crematoria and instead claimed it represented the mother's unconscious death wishes. According to Bettelheim, a baby in the crib is like a prisoner at Auschwitz. I imagine he must have been a deeply unhappy man for much of his life.

What you see is limited by what you know or believe, including false beliefs. For two years, I failed to see any signs that Ben's development was delayed or unusual. Or rather, I saw things but didn't connect them.

'It's just his character,' I thought when Ben suddenly refused to join in the swimming lessons we'd been doing each term for a year.

'He's just bored,' Robert said when Ben wandered off from the group at the library story time.

'It's too hard for him, he's cautious like me,' I said when he wouldn't join in the baby gym class.

'It's too noisy,' we agreed when he wouldn't play with the other kids at playgroup.

'He's just a bit slower than the other babies in learning to use a spoon and a straw,' we said when he struggled to feed himself. We saw he was different, but accepted his difference without concern or judgement. We were innocent. Ben had his eccentricities, but they were just part of him, his character, his personality. The story we told about Ben was that he was a happy, alert, intelligent and affectionate child.

But even then, another story was starting to manifest. Gradually, shafts of light were picking up a new narrative, as if written in invisible ink. I remember how I borrowed my sister Pauline's child-development book and checked every aspect of his development against it.

'Are you worried about something?' she asked. And I must have said no, and believed myself. Because I checked him and at eighteen months he was within the normal range in all aspects of his development. So I gave her back the book. Deep inside me, though, something was ticking; I was already thinking, there is something odd here.

Over the six months it took for Ben to be diagnosed with autism, this new story emerged, bit by bit. This story was about a child who was anxious and frustrated, needy for comfort but unable to reciprocate affection, who couldn't play, couldn't communicate and whose only interests were objects and numbers. I felt as though everything I previously thought about my son was mistaken. I no longer knew him. He no longer loved me – or rather, I felt that perhaps he had never loved me. In a way, I was rewriting history, viewing the past quite differently, feeling the ground beneath shift and buckle.

This, I think, is how grief works. When Ben started to change and move away from us, when he no longer looked at us or wanted to share things with us, when he even turned away from my touch in his sleep – at that time, I felt as though I had lost my child, the Ben I knew, or thought I knew. Because I had loved him for two years, I mourned that child, but I did so secretly and guiltily, because of course Ben had not died or disappeared. I had him still, but I felt that I had lost him. I mourned for several years. I put away every photograph of baby Ben in a drawer and locked them up. I tried never to think or talk about the past. The old Ben hid himself away in my heart, a kind of shadow twin to carry the loss I experienced each day. And I felt profoundly disloyal to my real child.

But over time, my shadow child gradually disintegrated and I allowed myself to be reunited with my real child once again. Ben – with all his differences – became once more the baby I recognised the moment I saw him, who gasped at the sea air, who woke every hour for comfort, who loved bright colours and feared loud noises. He was both the alert, happy, affectionate child and the anxious, frustrated, needy child. I could hold both stories about Ben in my mind and see that those two stories were not, after all, very different and that I had never lost my son, but simply learned more about him.

Although Ben's journey from birth to now has been different from the normal developmental pathway and he has not reached the expected milestones for his age, still, I can see now the continuity of both his wandering journey and his character. That is what matters to me now. His path is a roving, winding path that only he can take. And parenting him seems to mean that I, too, take a winding path and never really know

where I am going or what I should be doing next. I make mistakes all the time, but Ben wanders around me, ignoring my
errors and going his own way. Roaming.

THE CAGE

The eyes of others our prisons; their thoughts our cages.
—VIRGINIA WOOLF

'MUM, I NEED YOU,' sings a voice from the bedroom.

'I'm cooking, Ben. Can it wait?' I'm also reading a book as I stir the vegetables and I don't especially want to stop. After a pause, Ben replies, 'Not *really*,' meaning he wants me to come in now but he knows it isn't that urgent and so he's trying to be reasonable. I put the spoon and book onto the kitchen table and go into his room.

The rhythm of my days has changed. The things I considered interruptions have become, over the years, the fabric of my life and I no longer imagine a life without them. I have ceased to expect a life of smooth development and growth and instead expect stops and starts and changes and crises and regressions and plateaus and jumps.

The first interruption, I suppose, is the diagnosis. At the time, I did what I think of as 'the English thing'. I held grief close and dark, moved straight from discovery to action, modelled to everyone that this was not a huge derailment but just another little curve in the road. In other words, I lied. I put on the cheerful face of all those struck by sudden disasters, small or large, the face demanded by a world deeply threatened by loss, disfigurement, disability and the unknown.

And of course the discovery and naming of a disability like autism doesn't actually happen suddenly, like an accident, injury or the onset of an illness. It's just that we grasp such things in small, sudden moments that still cling to us years afterwards.

I arrive early and sit in 'the cage'. This is the name the staff at the autism therapy centre give to the parents' lounge, perhaps because of the metal bars of the childproof gate. It's not really a lounge, but a small space immediately to the right of the front door, with four cane chairs, a low coffee table and a box of grubby toys. Soon several other parents arrive and Jane, the clinical psychologist, invites us into a large room at the front of the building. We sit around a low grey craft table on small children's plastic chairs. Jessie, the educational psychologist, joins us. Jessie and Jane – their names seem partnered, but they are quite different. Jessie is beautiful, with orange crinkly hair, creamy skin, delicate features and that gently confident listening demeanour of the professional. Next to her, Jane looks plain. But I like Jane. It was she who let slip the term 'the cage'.

Jane welcomes us to the first parent training session of the year. She doesn't invite us to introduce ourselves. She asks us what we knew about autism before our children were diagnosed and what we know now. Without really answering her question, the women (we are all women here) start to tell their stories.

An Italian, very tanned, very elegant: 'The paediatrician said, Your daughter is autistic, and I just said, Oh, right, and left! I didn't know anything about it, but I just left.'

The woman next to her: 'I was the opposite. I argued. He

can't be, I said, because I thought all autistic kids just sat in a corner and screamed and banged their heads on the wall.' She laughs and we all smile, but they're anxious smiles – it could be our child who screams and bangs all day.

Other stories. 'I knew something was wrong but everyone said, Stop worrying, he'll grow out of it. Eventually, I was told he was autistic – that's when my world crumbled.' Her lower lip quivers.

'For me it was a relief.' This is a young woman with big dark eyes and a very ready smile. 'I said, Hurray, now I know what to do.' She's already told us that her daughter used to cry for hours non-stop and has several physical disabilities as well as autism. She speaks openly and laughs at herself. I am awed by her positive attitude (though I wonder what she is like when there is no one else around).

Only two of us have not told our diagnosis stories. There is a pause as people give us space to talk. I look across to the other woman who hasn't spoken. The lines on her face, like my grey hair, mark her out as older than most of the other mothers, forty-something not twenty-five or thirty. We smile at one another. We aren't going to tell how we felt when our child was diagnosed – not now, not here. We share not only our age, but also something else – the guilt of it, of being an older mother.

Unlike other mothers, I was slow to recognise that Ben's development was disordered. I think this was partly because he always had language – of a sort – and also because he exhibited signs of eccentricity from such a young age that I viewed them as character traits, not a condition with a name. But there were other reasons, too. Reasons to do with my own development, my own parenting – that cloudy past I had hardly considered for forty years. I had a two-year-old who counted to one hundred, didn't like being with other children, confused his pronouns and was afraid of loud noises, sudden movements, animals, cars, even the wind. These things didn't alarm me at first. Other things I just didn't notice, like his inability to follow a pointing finger or to see where I was looking and the fact he didn't know how to play like a child. My own beliefs and experiences of childhood blinded me to how unusual Ben's behaviour really was. We only know what we know.

Once I did realise Ben was too far from normal to be simply an eccentric, then the likely diagnosis became obvious to me immediately, in the strange way that dream images rise up in the night and stay with you ever after.

We are at my friend Karl's place. Karl's teenagers are looking after Ben and I'm talking to Karl. Ben comes and leans against my knees and starts flicking the on/off switch of the heater (it's May, so it isn't plugged in). I am telling Karl how, the day before, the director of Ben's day care centre told me that Ben wasn't playing with the other children and tended to sit on his own a lot.

'They think he's a bit odd,' I say in a jokey way, my anxiety clearly obvious to Karl, who just listens and nods. Ben begins turning the temperature knob on the heater, reading the numbers one to six. As he does so I hear myself say, 'Social inadequacy and love of numbers. It sounds like autism, doesn't it?' I'm amazed to have said this. I'm not aware of knowing anything about autism and no one has mentioned it to me. The word just seems to arrive in my mouth from nowhere.

Karl's face remains impassive. 'Well,' he says, 'we have a friend who has worked a lot with autistic children and she would be more than happy to talk to you about Ben, I'm sure. I'll give you her number.'

That is all. We talk of other things after that. But I see that Karl thinks Ben isn't normal. That night after Ben has gone to bed I do an internet search on autism. There are sites with a list of symptoms to look for in two-year-olds. Pronoun reversal, lack of interest in peers, lack of imaginative play, disordered language development – all of these fit Ben. Other symptoms are lack of affection, no language, signs of intellectual impairment, 'challenging' behaviour, unwillingness to be touched, no eye contact – these aren't like Ben at all. Surely that means he's not autistic, I tell myself. I close down the computer and stand. My body feels hollow and weightless, the ground uneven as I walk into the kitchen. I stand at the sink, waiting for someone to tell me what to do.

It will be six months before Ben is officially diagnosed. But tonight is the first time I allow myself to consider that Ben might be more than just eccentric, shy or a slow developer. This is the night the world starts slipping away behind frosted glass.

After my internet search, I went to see our doctor. He didn't know much about autism, but he agreed that some of my stories about Ben suggested a form of developmental delay and referred me to a developmental paediatrician. He suggested I write down my major concerns so that he could use them in his letter of referral. Ben was two and a half years old then. What I wrote down as my concerns were:

Lack of social skills – Ben doesn't relate to other children at all, or at most stands back and watches them.

Living in a world of his own – he seems to have a story running through his head all the time and spends hours just chatting and laughing to himself.

Language – he understands us but doesn't really communicate or engage in conversation.

Obsession – Ben loves numbers, sees them everywhere and loves to recite the times tables (heard on a CD).

Games – he has no interest in normal kids' activities such as drawing, playing with a ball, dressing up or make-believe games.

Biting – Ben hates biting into food and has trouble managing his mouth and tongue movements.

Looking at this list now, I realise that, in a way, I had already done the paediatrician's job. My summary is very close to the substance of the official diagnosis report. It shows the key areas of delay and disorder necessary for a diagnosis of autism, as outlined in the *DSM IV*: 'impairment in social interactions', 'impairment in communication' and 'restrictive and stereotyped patterns of behaviour and interests'. It also alludes to what I now know to be sensory integration and motor planning challenges (his difficulty in biting and eating).

What I also notice now, years later, is that Ben both has and hasn't changed. He is still recognisable as the boy who loves numbers, tells himself stories, has trouble planning and executing things and finds most children's activities pretty uninteresting.

It is me and my views that have most changed since then.

'Now, Ben, can you do this jigsaw puzzle for me?' asks Jim, the psychologist, placing a simple puzzle with four pieces in front of Ben. Ben quickly puts in the pieces and then stands up and starts to walk away from the table.

'Good work,' says Jim. 'Now sit down, Ben. Here's another one. Can you do this?'

'Look, Ben, it's numbers,' I say. Ben sits down and completes the puzzle while Jim times him, raising his eyebrow at the speed with which he finishes.

'Good work. Now this one, Ben.' It's a more complex one with eight pieces, all different shapes. Ben puts in seven pieces but struggles with the last one, holding it back to front and getting frustrated. Jim watches, his timer ticking away. Ben starts banging the piece against the board. I reach out to help him but Jim raises one hand and shakes his head at me. I have to remind myself that this is not a test; it's an opportunity for the psychologist to observe Ben and identify any developmental delays. Jim puts away the puzzles and gets out some coloured blocks. He gives one pile to Ben and keeps an identical pile on his side of the table. Then he places a red block in the middle of the table and asks Ben to do the same. Ben chooses a red block from his pile and moves it to the centre of the table.

'Good work, Ben. Now, can you match this?' asks Jim, putting a blue block on top of a yellow one. Ben copies him.

'Good work. Now this.' Jim has used four different colours this time, creating a stack with two blocks at the base and then two on top. Ben picks up a few blocks but doesn't lay them down.

'Ben, do the same,' prompts Jim. Ben hesitates.

'It's okay, darling, just have a go,' I say. He collects the correct four colours and puts them on the table in a pile.

'Is that the same, Ben?' asks Jim. 'Can you make yours the same?' But it seems that Ben can't. The task is too complicated for him. He seems to know that he hasn't yet created a mirror image of Jim's blocks but he doesn't know how to do so. He touches the blocks, but doesn't move them. His face is blank of all emotion. There is a pause and then Jim says, 'Okay, let's do something else now. Why don't you have a hug with Mum while I get out some other toys?' Ben backs towards me until my arms are around him. Jim writes some notes in his little book.

This was part of one of the eight assessments that formed the diagnosis process. About half of the assessments involved a paediatric professional observing Ben; the rest were interviews with me. In these interviews I was asked many questions. Every corner of Ben's development and behaviour was turned inside out and scrutinised against the hard white light of 'normal'.

Was the pregnancy normal? What about the delivery? Was Ben a healthy baby? Could he breastfeed? How did he sleep?

How did he sleep? I give them the short answer – not easily, not well, not much.

When did he first sit up? Crawl? Eat with a spoon? When did he say his first words? Put two words together? What about three words?

I don't remember; I haven't kept a proper record.

Does he point? Does he drag you around by the arm? How does he get what he wants? If you're upset, does he recognise that? What does he do?

I'm not sure. I don't allow myself to appear upset in front of Ben. Is this odd of me, I suddenly wonder?

Well, if you're in a park or somewhere and another child falls and cries, how does Ben react?

I can't think. It must have happened but I can't remember. Did I ignore the other child just as Ben did? He's asking about empathy, whether Ben feels empathy.

Let's talk about play. What does Ben like to play with? Does he play with parts of toys like the wheels of a car or whole toys?

'Whole toys,' I say, in relief. 'He never just spins the wheels.'

How does he play with cars, then?

I falter. He doesn't really play, I know that. He lines them up, he names them, he carries them around. But he never, ever pushes them along the floor, pretending they are driving along a road.

The questions go on, exposing every deficit, every strangeness. My role changes. I am no longer the delighting mother, but the spectator who judges – is that normal or disordered, delayed, dysfunctional? His strange behaviours are no longer endearing eccentricities – they have officially become developmental deficits, signs of autism.

It is our third and last visit to Dr P, the paediatrician. We sit in the waiting room, between a collection of broken toys and a table with a few torn cartoon-character books. Ben (now almost three) wanders around, quoting from a video he watched last night. Dr P says hello to me, then motions us into her office. We sit – she at her desk and I in a stiff-backed yellow vinyl chair. Ben goes straight to the height chart on the wall. Dr P opens the file and reads the reports from the psychologist and speech pathologist. I wait. A strange smirk appears to cross her face as she tells me that, yes, Ben will be diagnosed as having an Autism Spectrum Disorder. I'm not surprised. I've done my homework. I was expecting this. I ask, 'What happens now?' and Dr P says, 'I'll do a report and send a copy to the Disability Services Commission and they'll contact you.'

'What should we be doing?' I ask. 'We've started speech therapy but what else should I do?'

'Speech therapy is a good idea,' she answers.

'Should we have any more tests? For hearing problems or epilepsy perhaps?'

'I don't think they're necessary.'

I wait. I want some sort of prognosis, something about the future. She closes the file.

'Should we come back to you in six months or a year to assess his progress?' I'm desperate now; I don't want to leave without something beyond a diagnosis.

'No need,' she says, and stands. (Our time is up.) 'You'll get my report,' she says as she opens the door.

'Thank you. Come on, Benji, we're going now.' He comes and stands beside me. 'Say goodbye,' I say.

'Bye,' says Ben, looking at the floor.

'Goodbye,' she says to me.

I pay the receptionist, take Ben's hand and open the front door. We stand for a moment, our eyes adjusting to the bright light flashing off the cars passing on Colin Street. We step into the glittering spring air, together, alone.

This, I think, was the moment when I should have gone home and taken to my bed. I should have done what I call 'the American thing'– called my closest friends and family, told them the news, cried for a week in bed and let others look after us. Perhaps if I had done this the next few years would have been easier. But the public expression of grief was unknown to me – still is, in fact. I didn't know then that we need to celebrate losses as much as gains; that rituals are required to help us live experiences like this rather than just get through them. Instead I held Ben's hand very tightly and we went to a café with a sunny courtyard where I drank coffee and Ben walked around eating an apple and looking at the table numbers. That was our solace.

I have been reading *Out of Africa* by Karen Blixen and come across a story that she says was told to her as a child. It goes like this. A man who lived by a pond was woken one night by a loud noise. He went out and ran towards the pond, but in the darkness, running back and forth, guided only by the noise, he stumbled and fell often. At last he found a leak in the dam and plugged the leak before going to bed. The next morning, looking out of his upstairs window, he saw with surprise that his footprints had traced the figure of a stork on the ground.

The real point of the story, I suppose, is the gift given to the man at the end. He saw his own story. His frenzied and haphazard running back and forth became a design of beauty and significance.

Some people may see motherhood as an act encompassing beauty and significance. In some ways it is. The experience of it, however, is much more like the man running in the dark, trying to follow a noise. I didn't think much about the future, the shape of things to come, until I found myself holding Ben's hand, standing before a word that howled past us like a great wind. Autism. What it meant was unclear, but the crack of the wind echoes in my ears even now.

This wasn't just another little curve in the road, an interruption that could soon be recovered from. I know that now. It was an interruption that moved us both into a new space, a space where interruptions are the norm, the very rhythm of our life.

Having a child with a developmental disability means you live with disruptions – part of the condition is that typical development does not occur. The structures of society, however, continue to be ordered around the typical, or perhaps ideal, developmental path and so there are continual pauses and reconfigurations in your life. In a sense, you live against the story told by society. There is a kind of silencing that happens when your own story (or your child's) is fragmented, disordered and out of sequence with the typical story. You can't share your stories in the same way as other parents.

'The questions he asks, honestly, it's amazing. He said the other day, "Mum, is there a plug at the bottom of the sea, just like in the bath?"' says Sita.

90

'Oh yes, Mel's the same. It's "why, why, why" all the time now,' says Laura.

Ben and I and Laura and her two children are at Sita's house. The mums are drinking tea and the kids are playing together, except Ben, who is wandering around the house looking at things and talking to himself. Ben is the same age as Mel, but he hasn't got to 'why' questions yet. We're still on 'what is that?' and naming things.

Kamal, Sita's son, runs in and says, 'Mum, can we get the bikes out?'

'Yes of course,' says Sita, 'Ben, Mel and Joe can take it in turns to ride the three-wheeler trike.'

'Ben won't,' I say. 'He can't ride yet.'

'Oh.' She goes out to help the children with the bikes and soon they are racing around the garden on wheels, even Joe, the youngest, having a turn on the trike. Sita makes more tea.

'How's it been, going back to work?' I ask Laura.

'Oh, it's fine. They have two days at childcare and one day with Mum. They love that. When they're at Mum's place, I ring them at lunchtime. Mel really likes talking on the phone now.'

'That's nice.'

'Yes, she's so sweet. She always says, "I love you, Mummy" at the end of the conversation.'

I look at Laura's glowing face and I see that she has no idea how this story might affect me. She wouldn't know that Ben has never said 'I love you' to me. I might have told her he cries bitterly every time I leave him with anyone else, but she probably forgot. She certainly wouldn't realise that he doesn't understand the concept of talking to someone he can't see over the phone. Sita starts talking about the pretend phone calls her two have, the way they mimic her phone manner.

These are two of my best friends, women I have known for twenty years and who had their children around the same time as I did. They are thoughtful, caring women. And their children are charming and good-natured children. Still, here I am, feeling as though I don't belong. And there is Ben, wandering about on his own, ignored by everyone. Where is the space for our stories?

Arthur Frank says of illness and disability narratives that 'Telling an interrupted life requires a new kind of narrative.' The illness story, he says, begins in wreckage. The story is interrupted and is about interruption. These are uncomfortable stories without tidy endings, and this is the story I want to tell. A story about a boy who can't bear to leave his mother's side, but who ignores her much of the time they are together. A story about a boy who is still learning at three what other children learned in their first year of life. A story about a boy who may never tell his mother he loves her.

This is what I thought, because back then I didn't realise that Ben would grow and learn and develop and that he would, one day, have the impulse to tell me he loved me.

The 'wreckage' Frank discusses shatters our coherent sense of life's sequence and, with it, our sense of memory: memories remain 'unassimilated fragments that refuse to become past'. This, perhaps, is why one remembers so well those moments of the diagnosis – the way Dr P seemed to smirk, the bright light of the cars, the moment you realise you are alone after all.

Two months after Ben's third birthday, the letter from the Disability Services Commission comes. I am impatient. I want the formalities over. I want to start getting therapy for Ben. To know where we stand. (Of course, I do know where we stand – on the edge, in the howling wind.) I open the envelope:

As you are aware, a referral was received for Benjamin by the Commission from Dr P. I wish to advise that the diagnosis of autism has been accepted, and that Benjamin is eligible for the Commission's Early Intervention Program. You will shortly be contacted by your Local Area Coordinator.

I hear the crackling as the letter shakes in my hand, see the print blurring and enlarging, feel a shudder in my chest. I remember a friend who cried when he finally received his divorce papers.

'But you wanted the divorce,' I'd said, puzzled.

'It's still an ending,' he'd replied.

But this is not an ending, nor a beginning. It just feels like one.

BONUS

Too many have dispensed with generosity in order to practise charity.—ALBERT CAMUS

I'M THINKING OF A long weekend in Margaret River and a heater for the lounge room. I'm thinking of a new bicycle for Ben. I'm thinking of a visit to my favourite bookshop, dinner and an evening at the theatre, a new pair of boots. I'm having these thoughts because I've just been given $600. Fantasising is what you do. But I'm thinking these things also as a way of drowning out that small but persistent discomfort that has been droning away in the background ever since I got the letter. It's from the Minister for Families, Housing and Community Services.

Dear Ms Robertson

The Government recognises the important role and contribution you make as a carer. Carers perform a vital role in our community in caring for the aged and people with disabilities. As part of the Australian Government's 2008–09 Budget, eligible carers will be provided with a bonus payment. You are entitled to the 2008 one-off bonus payment of $600.

Why is it that I feel slightly soiled when I read this? Is it the clinical tone of the letter, the fact that it confirms what we all know anyhow, that individual families must look after their own, that taxpayers and governments don't 'perform this vital role'? The bonus is a kind of gift or reward, perhaps, not because I'm doing a good job (who would know whether I am?) or because I've chosen to do this job of caring, but just because I'm an 'eligible carer'.

The term bonus was originally stock-exchange slang. It means 'a boon or gift over and above what is normally due' and 'a premium for services rendered or expected'. But at times it has been used to mean a bribe. Perhaps that is the more appropriate usage here – not a reward for good behaviour (that is, accepting the caring role) but a bribe to ensure that good behaviour continues.

What did I expect – that society might suddenly value caring for the disabled? Perhaps my discomfort is because this letter codifies my status as a recipient of government funds, officially classifies me as 'carer'? It's a strange thing to be described as a 'carer' of my own son. He is nine years old. I am his mother. This shift from 'mother' to 'carer' makes me profoundly uneasy.

To use the term carer about the mother of a young child is to mark her out as different from other mothers. Not that she cares more or less for her child, but rather that her role is not the seemingly simple and socially valued role of mothering one's own child but a more complex and invisible one of providing life-long care for a child who may never become independent. That the life-long care is limited by the mother's life expectancy, not her child's, is another anomaly of the role.

Carer is a recently coined word, probably first used in 1978 to describe a person whose paid or unpaid role is to care for the sick, aged or disabled. But it carries the weight of six centuries of use in English of the term 'care' to describe not only 'taking care' but also 'to sorrow, mourn, lament' or 'be troubled by' something. There is implicit in the term a sense of burden as well as of love.

Does the term carer imply that there is something unnatural in the mother's relationship to her son, that because the normal developmental path of the child has been disrupted the relationship must be redefined? What we find most appealing about children – their vulnerable dependency on us – becomes problematic and disturbing in adults. So much so that we have to give a name to people who provide daily assistance to vulnerable or dependent adults. They are no longer mother, father, spouse, son or daughter; they are 'carer'. And the person they assist is no longer son, daughter, spouse or parent; they are the 'care-recipient'. The relationship is constructed and defined as unequal – giver and recipient – in the way that the relationship between a parent and her non-disabled child is not, even though the dynamic of dependence is the same.

We know that our society valorises independence over dependence, non-disabled people over people with a disability. I wonder if a similar privileging is happening in the distinction between mother and carer? Mothers of children with a disability are often told, 'You're doing a wonderful job,' and 'I couldn't do it,' and 'I really admire you.' Although people mean well when they make these comments, the somewhat patronising tone suggests they speak from a position of assumed superiority as well as from a deep-seated fear of disability. In spite of people's best intentions, I often sense that the mother of a disabled child, like the child, is seen by other mothers as damaged.

Now I think of it, I have never used the term carer about myself, even though I have ticked that box on the various government forms that I have had to complete over the years. I'm a member of Carers Australia and support the political and educational work that carers' associations undertake. Yet I am still ambivalent about the word.

I am reminded here of the French philosopher Louis Althusser and his concept of 'hailing' or 'interpellation'. The individual is singled out and identified – 'hailed' – by society or its institutions. In recognising herself as the one hailed, she allows herself to be cast in a particular role. To be hailed is to be encouraged or coerced into thinking of oneself as what society defines one to be. By receiving a diagnosis of autism, my son was hailed by medical practice – he became 'boy with autism' rather than just 'boy'. At the same time, I seem to have been hailed as 'carer' and my response, of course, was to accept that identification. Althusser's argument is that the function of religion, medicine, education, law, culture and politics is to make such labels appear to be self-evident truths. An individual internalises the identity offered to her, while still believing she is making a free choice. We do what we are expected to do, what institutions require of us.

In fact, I think individuals both accept and resist these identifications. Identity is plural and changing – a process of becoming that shifts throughout our lives. When I experience that dissonance between my role as carer and my own sense of myself as mother, I am renegotiating my identity. I may not want or be able to renegotiate my role – how many carers are going to abandon their loved one at the local hospital or police station? – but I am reworking my sense of how that role confines and defines me.

Of course, parent or carer, I'm still happy to have the $600! For the parent of an autistic child, this money represents four sessions with a clinical psychologist, or six sessions of occupational or speech therapy. Given that children my son's age usually need at least one hour per week of psychology, speech and occupational therapy, this money won't last long in most families.

'Is $600 a lot of money?' asks Ben.

'Well, it's quite a lot,' I reply.

'Enough to buy a house?'

'Oh no, Ben. A house costs a lot more.'

'How about a computer?' he suggests.

'Well, maybe half a computer. That wouldn't be much use, would it?' I joke.

'You could buy a lot of Thomas the Tank Engines with $600.'

'Yes, you could,' I agree. In fact, we could probably buy around thirty of them, which would certainly make Ben happy.

'Maybe we could buy a new one, then?'

'Well, we have a lot already.' I'm still contemplating the bike and the heater, but in reality I'm fairly sure our bonus will be spent on occupational therapy sessions to help Ben learn the skills to play with his peers instead of Thomas the Tank.

'But we don't have Lady or Mavis,' points out Ben, 'and they are girl-engines. You'll like them.'

'Oh, I see. Well, maybe we will get one more then.' I'm impressed by Ben's reasoning and persuasive skills. At least I don't have to pay for speech therapy any more!

Once, not long ago, I was a successful consultant, earning a living wage. I had a level of autonomy and control over my life and some influence over my future and, in a small way, on state government policy in the area of my consultancy work.

My downshifting started when I moved in with Robert, an artist rich in talent, not money. I left a nearly new two-bedroom villa in a suburb by the sea in order to move into a 1950s weatherboard house in need of renovation in an area full of social housing. In those days, it was a suburb that raised people's eyebrows. 'Is it safe?' they would ask.

Is anywhere safe?

Over time, as I moved from mother to carer-who-doesn't-call-herself-a-carer, I downshifted yet again. My job went from full time to part time, so that I could spend more time with Ben. The renovation plans went out the door. The proposed family trip around Australia in a campervan was postponed indefinitely. Then the marriage disappeared on us. So here I am, a single mother, living in a yet-to-be-renovated sky-blue house with a garden that is untamed and a child who has most of my attention.

Our marriage didn't end because Ben is autistic. He has a devoted father, who is still very present in his life. It probably failed for all the usual reasons. But perhaps we let it go slightly more easily than other people do because of our preoccupation with Ben. To my mind, a marriage break-up is a minor setback compared with finding out your son has a lifelong disability. I'm guessing that Robert would feel the same. Our marriage seemed so unimportant compared with what our son was experiencing that it withered away in a few years. That's part of the story, anyway.

In her book *Ordinary Time*, Nancy Mairs says that one of the main consequences of experiencing disability as a result of her multiple sclerosis is 'the loneliness felt by anybody whose life unfolds out of sync with general social patterns'. When a child's life unfolds out of sync, both parent and child can feel that loneliness. The space in which I work and live and socialise is very small because I have stopped doing things that are too difficult or demanding to do with or around Ben. Working full days, for example, means that someone else must drop Ben off to school and pick him up and take care of him for two or three hours before I get home from work. This is possible but it comes at a cost, resulting in much more anxiety and distress for Ben. Since getting through the school day is hard enough as it is, I don't want to make things more challenging for him. And then for me to find someone who can relate well to Ben and is free to take care of him for a reasonable cost is much harder than it is for parents of typically developing children. I can't just enrol him in occasional care or long day care and expect him and the childcare workers to cope.

Social events are proscribed in the same way. My first thoughts are whether Ben will manage in a particular environment. Anything noisy or crowded is out. Anything involving interaction with unknown children is out. Anything that demands more than a ten-minute attention span is out. Anything that involves sitting down is out. And so on. When we do go to a social event I spend all my time on the margins with Ben, encouraging him to interact, helping him feel safe, trying to prevent him from leaving within half an hour of our arriving. We always do leave first, of course, usually just before the main event we have come to enjoy. We are the Houdinis of social life – always escaping at the eleventh hour.

Ben's life is played out in a small space, too. He goes to the local school (and has a part-time education assistant there), but he can't manage any mainstream recreational activities. The children at school play with him sometimes, but he rarely gets invited to birthday parties or out-of-school activities. After school, he unwinds at home with me or attends his therapy appointments. On the weekends, he spends time with me or his father, going to a park or a swimming pool or playing with his Thomas the Tank Engines. Sometimes he sees other family members or friends who know how to relate to him. He's not unhappy – this is life as he knows it. In fact, one of the joys of parenting Ben is that he is generally a very happy child.

I'm not unhappy either, but I recognise that I have moved into a kind of ghetto. Just as I have shifted from mother to carer, so too have I moved from consumer to client, taxpayer to recipient, citizen to outsider. In truth, I am still a consumer (I buy things like everyone else) and I do still pay taxes (though not as much as I used to) but my point is that I don't feel like that any more. Because I get a carer's allowance of fifty dollars per week and these vexed one-off bonuses, because I get letters from the government telling me that I have to inform them of any changes in my circumstances, because I am on the Centre-link database and have the feeling of being watched by govern-ment, my sense of being an autonomous, independent citizen with freedom of speech and action is unravelling. I am con-stantly negotiating with state institutions (hospitals, schools, government agencies) to actually receive the services that Ben is eligible for, rather than simply being on their list of eligible families. Even though it is my son's right under law to receive assistance, for example, to ensure his participation at school, I have to continually advocate for him to ensure that this occurs. This is true for all the parents of children with disabilities that I've met; it's not about me, or Ben, but the system. This feeling of exclusion from the main institutions of the state contributes to my sense of living as an outsider.

There is a concept in anthropology called 'liminality'. In traditional societies, a person moves into 'liminal space' as part of a rite of passage marking a transition from one socially val-ued role to another – for example in puberty, during preg-nancy or through illness. A rite of passage normally includes three stages: separation, liminality and reincorporation. The disability scholar Robert Murphy has used 'liminality' to describe the place of people with disabilities in Western society. For someone suffering an acute illness, the return home from hospital and successful convalescence mark his or her return to normal life and status. But for people with chronic illness or disability, that return may never happen. They may find themselves relegated to a kind of permanent liminality. They cannot be 'cured' and reincorporated into society, and so death may appear the only symbolic way to reintegrate them.

As a parent, I feel that I have fallen into liminal space with Ben. What Michael Bérubé calls the 'social apparatus' of disability surrounds and engulfs the parent as much as the child. And the consequences of disability can be significant for parents, too. Unemployment, poverty, social isolation, scrutiny of your behaviour by professional experts, objectification by others – all of this happens to parents as well as to their disabled children.

I often experience the sense that Ben and I are separate from ordinary life; that we stand on the sidelines watching other people live normally while our lives move in slow motion. We do this literally, of course, at every sports day at school, when all the children except Ben participate in team sports and running races. When he does participate in group activities, as in the school dance class, I see that Ben is doing all the actions five seconds after the other children and in a way that is slightly exaggerated, as if he is performing a parody of the others. Sometimes I wonder if my life has become a parody of motherhood, performing tasks for my child long after he would normally be able to do them himself.

Liminality, of course, may also be a place of transformation. In this in-between space, individuals can develop alternative social arrangements and question the status quo. We can do it as individuals – living our lives in ways that suit us, not others.

But can we also do this as a group? If I were able to embrace my identity as 'carer', could I be part of a group that challenges the notion that individual families and not taxpayers must be responsible for the majority of the caring work in our society? Could we identify the key roles that money and health play in granting individuals citizenship? Is it possible that Ben, at eighteen years of age, will consider himself citizen not outsider, consumer not client?

'How old will I be when you die?' asks Ben. We have just driven past Fremantle Cemetery and I suppose this has triggered his question.

'Well, we don't know, Ben. But I'm hoping to live for quite a while yet!'

'If you die when you are eighty, I will be ... umm ... forty-four.'

'That's right, yes,' I agree.

'But, who will look after me when you die?'

'Well, you might be able to look after yourself then. Forty-four is quite old.' Ben looks unconvinced but makes no comment.

The notion of death has changed for me. I can no longer contemplate that I may ever die. Like thousands of other mothers across this country, I have no faith that my son will be cared for without me. I look at the most vulnerable people in our society and I see that we fail them miserably. What is to be done?

'Mum,' says Ben, 'when you die, I'll make a plaque for you, like in the cemetery.'

'That's nice. What will it say?'

'Your name and the dates you were born and died and suchlike.'

'Oh yes. Anything else?' I ask. He thinks for a moment.

'She was a good mother. Sadly missed. RIP. RIP means rest in peace,' Ben explains.

'Great. I like that, Ben. And where will this plaque go, I wonder?'

'Remember when we buried the hermit crabs?' asks Ben.

'Yes, in the garden, wasn't it?'

'Yes, I think you'll go with them, in the compost bin. And the plaque will go on top.'

I can't help laughing at this. It's the story of my life: here am I agonising about life and death while Ben cuts straight to the chase. I will end up in the compost bin eventually, however much this worries me. In the meantime, I'm touched that he intuitively grasps my attempt to be a good mother – not a fantastic mother or a super-mum or a special mother of a special child, but just a 'good enough' mother.

'Mum,' says Ben, 'when we get home, we might play with the Thomas the Tank Engines.'

'Good idea, Ben. I'd like to do that.'

There is always the Island of Sodor, where steamies are Really Useful, diesels are naughty and the Fat Controller is king.

GEOMETRY OF ECHOES

And always, in our daydreams, the house is a large cradle.
—GASTON BACHELARD

ROBERT AND I SIT at the kitchen table while Ben plays a computer game in the next room. My right elbow rests near the darkened ring I made years ago when I put down a hot casserole dish to answer the phone. Further round is a chip in the bevelled edge, caused by the side of a ladder Robert was carrying after he retrieved a dead rat from the roof space. There are plenty of texta marks, too, where Ben's scribbles have overshot his paper. The table is now in Robert's new house – or rather, the house he is renting from our friend Janet.

'The house looks quite good now, with furniture and everything,' I say. 'Given it was rented out for a decade I'm surprised it's in such reasonable shape.'

'There's a few dodgy lights and so on. But it's okay.'

In the pause that follows, we hear a character from Ben's computer game singing in an American accent.

'I'd forgotten the colourful paintwork here,' I say. 'Cheerful, isn't it? Especially the lounge room with the blue and gold.'

'I like it,' says Robert. 'Remember when we danced in that room? When was it?'

'Thirteen years ago.' It was when we first met, through Janet.

'Thirteen years! Gone, just like that!' says Robert, waving his arm over the table. We sit in silence for a while and I imagine the story of our marriage and separation laid between us on the table, taking very little space, leaving only cracks and marks behind. And Ben, of course.

'He's been alright, then?' asks Robert, jerking his head towards Ben.

'He's been fine. Just as usual, really.'

Robert nods. 'He's a tough kid.'

When we first told Ben that we were separating, we didn't even use that word. I just said that Mum and Dad had decided we would each have our own house and that Dad would be moving into his new house in a few days.

'Will I live alone until New Year's Day?' asked Ben.

We reassured him that he would always be with one of us. Then he wanted to know all about Dad's new house and go to visit it. I'd prefaced this conversation by saying to Ben that we had to tell him something that might shock and upset him, but he hadn't seemed shocked or upset.

'It isn't real yet,' I said afterwards.

'He's hiding his feelings,' replied Robert.

The next morning, Ben came into my bed and said, 'I'm too sad to go to school today. All I can think about is this two-house business.'

'I understand,' I said. 'It's very hard, this sort of change. But don't worry, Mum and Dad will still be with you lots.'

'I'm too sad to go to school,' Ben insisted.

'I'm sorry, but you still have to go to school, Ben.'

'What if I'm naughty because all I can think about is this two-house business?'

'I'll talk to the teachers. It'll be okay.' I thought he would argue more, but he obviously knew he wouldn't be able to skip school so he dropped the idea and went to watch a video. I noticed he chose a cartoon version of Hansel and Gretel.

As we walked to school, Ben asked me, 'Do you have anything to tell me today that will shock me?'

'No, Ben,' I said. 'I won't be shocking you today.'

Ben was at school the day Robert moved out. When I collected him from school, I reminded him that Dad had moved out and that he had taken a lot of furniture.

'Has the sofa gone?' asked Ben. He's always loved jumping on that sofa.

'Yes, I'm sorry, darling. Dad's taken that to his new house.'

'Oh, good,' said Ben. 'Now I can play in the space behind it.'

Today is Ben's first overnight stay at Robert's house. I told him he could take with him anything he wanted, so we came loaded with three bags of Thomas the Tank Engine toys. For the last six months, they've been his favourites. As soon as we arrived at Robert's house, Ben put the Thomas engines in his bedroom, then ran into the garden to play in a jungle of nasturtiums and weeds, before going to use the computer.

'I think he'll like it here,' I say.

'Yes, he will,' agrees Robert.

We've started agreeing a lot.

'I'll leave you to it, then,' I suggest. Robert nods, so I say goodbye to Ben and drive home. For the first time, I walk into an empty house, knowing that Ben will be spending two nights with Robert. It's 5.15 p.m. on a Friday night and I can do whatever I like until Sunday morning. I sit in the lounge room (which now has only one chair in it) and stare at the wall. Invisible waves of pressure strike me. I didn't expect this. I thought I would feel relief now that Robert has finally moved out and we can move on from the failed negative space between us. I thought I would be glad to have some solitary time, free from the demands of husband and child. Instead, I am in pain. I desperately want Ben back here with me. My body feels hollow and fleshless. I try to make sense of this. I remind myself that I want Ben to spend time with Robert; it's a good thing. But it feels wrong. Eight years old is too young for a boy to leave home. The grief I feel is the primitive feeling of a mother animal when her cub is torn from her body.

Darkness opens in front of me as I realise the enormity of what I have done. I have taken away Ben's home.

What is home? Is it the place we live, the body of our mother, a myth? Is it, as Edward Relph says, 'the foundation of our identity as individuals and as members of a community, the dwelling-place of being'? If it is this 'irreplaceable centre of significance', how can we help our children feel at home in their world? Does a parent have to belong first in order to help her child belong?

Although I use the term home to describe the house I live in, I use it only in the most everyday sense. 'I'm off home now,' I say when I leave work, or 'I've got a copy at home,' about a book someone wants to borrow. I never think of my house as Home (with a capital), just the place I live. And although Perth has been my place of residence for the past twenty years, I don't feel a huge sense of attachment to it. I like living here, appreciate its beauty and benefits, like being near family and friends and having a good quality of life on a lowish income, but I don't feel a strong connection to the place or the landscape. I've always thought of myself as someone, not exactly homeless, but without a homeland, as if I'm missing the bit of self that other people have that binds them closely and deeply to a geographical place.

Home in the sense of a structure or geographical place is familiar to me. Home as a complex, deeply resonant psychic space that connects to geography – that sense of home has always been puzzling to me. Puzzling in the sense that I never really felt 'at home' in one place more than any other, though at the same time I recognise that I feel a type of homesickness every autumn. Can you be nostalgic only for a season of your childhood and not for the place or time itself? Is that nostalgia evidence of connection to a home?

When Simone Weil declares that 'To be rooted is perhaps the most important and least recognised need of the human soul', I half-agree, half-rebel. I imagine it must be powerful to have a strong sense of roots, a felt connection to and continuity with a family or community in time and place. But then isn't this notion of roots, of a home and homeland, responsible for causing a great deal of conflict and distress around the world? The more mobile our society is, the more the idea of home as a source of identity seems resonant. The greater the exile, the more significant becomes the notion of return.

I've come here before, in my dreams. I've walked along the final block of this cul de sac, past our special tree (gone now, or at least I don't recognise it), and stood staring up at the house. Heavy and dark, its shadow falling across me, cooling the air. In my dreams, I have seen the blackberries growing wild along the low front fence, the forget-me-nots lining the path to the front door. I have held up my hand, as if to knock on the wood, and waited. But in my dreams I don't enter the house. I turn from it – or perhaps the house turns from me.

I've come here before in waking life, too. We moved in soon after I turned two, left when I was ten to emigrate to Australia. That's old enough to have clear memories, but in fact they aren't clear, they are cloudy, incoherent, shapeless visions of a time that must have happened to someone else. Returning, for the first time in thirty-five years, I wondered how much I would remember about this house and small English village.

Earlier this afternoon, glimpses of barns, redbrick houses and silver-trunked trees shot through the bus windows like arrows. I couldn't say I recognised this place, but it moved me. An unidentified part of my body started aching. After twenty minutes, the driver nodded to me – this was Keele Village. I stood. The bus door opened. And I stepped out into the smell of my childhood. A powerful odour of woodland plants, mud, cow dung and damp air swept into my body and tossed me back in time, so that I stood by the roadside once more a child. There was the field where we fed the horses. There was the village church. There was the village green. And there, at the edge of the green, was a pedestrian crossing, the black and white striped poles topped by orange spheres, like large lollipops. One of the lights wasn't working. As I looked at the zebra crossing, with its lopsided flashing, it was as if nothing had changed. The very same lights – one working, one broken – had been waiting all these decades for me to return and cross the road once more.

Would I know the way to our old house from here? I wasn't sure. I had a map in my rucksack, but I decided to give my feet the chance to find their own way. And they did, taking me along Station Road and then left at The Oaks and up a path to Church Plantation, the name of our road. So that I am standing here at the corner near number five, ready to walk the final stretch to our house, number one.

Everything is new. Everything is familiar. It is as though I have never been here and yet have always been standing here by the row of silver birches on Church Plantation, about to enter my own childhood. I walk towards the front door. The blackberries and forget-me-nots are gone. The front garden is now a neat grassy area, with none of the wildness I remember (if it is memory, and not dreams or imagination). The door, too, has changed. It is no longer the heavy ornate black and gold door of my memory but modern and painted green, with a gold stick-on number one and a buzzer instead of the lion's head knocker. The bricks around it are the same, though, creating a strange decorative entrance. My hand shakes as I ring the bell.

The door is opened by a teenage boy with white hair.

'Hi,' I say. 'My name is Rachel. I used to live here forty years ago and I was wondering if you would mind if I took a few pictures of the house and garden, maybe had a look inside the house. I'm sorry if I've come at a bad time.'

''s okay. I'm sick today, that's why I'm home.'

'I'm sorry if I got you up.'

'You can come in,' he says and wanders back into the house, leaving the door open. I follow him in.

'It's changed a lot in forty years,' I say. 'Not surprising.'

The young man doesn't answer, just leans against a door-frame, looking uninterested but not annoyed. I look around the ground floor. The walls have been painted, the floors carpeted, the windows replaced. There is a modern kitchen and laundry – no sign of the old scullery – and the wall between the dining room and living room has been knocked down, creating a larger, differently shaped space. The three French doors have been removed and an extension like a sunroom has been added, incorporating some of what used to be the back garden. My mother's study has been turned into a home gym. I can see from all the clothes and gear around that several teenagers live in this house, as well as their parents. There is the stuff of modern life everywhere, making the house seem quite unlike the hollow, echoing place of my childhood. Between the kitchen and the study/gym, I see three stone steps down to the cloakroom.

These I remember. I stop and take a surreptitious photograph of my feet on the top step. Once down the steps, to the left there is still a toilet (though not the same toilet) and to the right a washbasin and a space for hanging coats. This room is immediately recognisable: in four decades it has hardly changed.

Several weeks later, when I show my family the photographs of our old house, they laugh at this one of my blue-shoed feet and three cream stone steps.

'What on earth did you take that for?' asks one sister.

'Oh, the downstairs bathroom,' says another. 'The steps used to be red tile, didn't they?'

My mother says, 'I remember when you were two, you used to sit on those steps and cry when I went to the toilet. You didn't even like being that distance from me.'

And my youngest sister says, 'Ah. That room, where we could go for privacy,' in tones that suggest that for her, too, that room was powerful.

It's true I went there sometimes just for privacy – a bathroom is a good place to be alone in a family of seven when bedrooms are shared. But entering the room was always a chilling experience. It was cold in there with the stone (or was it red tiled?) floor and no central heating or sunshine. And it smelt slightly dank and musty from the coats and boots in the corner. It was the last sort of room you would ever imagine wanting to retreat to, and yet I did. It was in this room as a young child, sitting on the toilet, running my fingers along the mortar lines between the cream tiles on the wall, that I dreamed of adventure, of magical creatures, of finding a passage to a world like C.S. Lewis's Narnia. I was always sure that this room, this cold, unforgiving nothing-place, would be the site of transformation.

Even then, I had some notion that you had to pass through the chilly dark places in order to enter the world of colour, the world I saw in books and wanted to have for myself, the mythic world of idyllic childhood.

If home, like childhood, is part myth, then it is surely a double-edged myth. There is the idea of home as nurturing and protective and there is the idea of home as a place of confinement and darkness. 'Our house is our corner of the world,' says Gaston Bachelard. The house of our childhood is inscribed in us, he says, in 'a passionate liaison of our bodies, who do not forget, with an unforgettable house'. The body of images that constitute our original house give us an illusion of stability, a place of refuge, a concentration of intimacy. Surely this notion of intimacy and refuge is dependent on a nurturing mother or carer? Is it not the interplay of the house and the mother's nurture that creates a home?

And what about the dark side of home, the house as a huge echoing place of empty shadows and impenetrable secrets? This, I think, has been many people's experience of home. How does this affect our experiences of belonging?

For women, perhaps, there is another dimension to the myth of a home. As children they may have witnessed their own mother's responsibility for caring for house and family and understood, at some level, the burden this responsibility entails. In my teenage and young adult years I was sure that having children would enslave me. Later, I began to think that my generation could have children but still be autonomous and liberated. It wasn't until I had Ben that I realised the complexities of the relationship between mothering and autonomy. It took experience, also, to teach me that the act of caring for another is a gift to oneself as much as to the other.

*

Ben appears to be taking our separation in his stride, but still I worry about him. He seems to get upset or irritated more easily than usual.

'Ben,' I ask him before school, 'are you worried or upset about anything to do with having two houses? Or do you feel that two houses is too much work?'

'No,' he replies, looking puzzled.

'Would you tell Dad or me if you were confused about things or if two houses were too tricky?' I ask.

'No.'

'Oh,' I say. 'Well, I'll rephrase that. Ben, I'd really like you to talk to me or Dad or someone else if you ever felt worried about anything. Could you do that?'

'Okay,' he says, as he wanders into his bedroom, clearly not interested in the conversation.

After a short while, Ben comes back into the kitchen. 'Mum, I want to ask you something important.'

'Sure,' I say, thinking he is going to talk about how he feels after all.

'If Percy and Thomas had a race, who do you think would win?'

'Oh,' I say, 'who do *you* think would win?'

'I think Thomas would.'

'I expect you're right, Ben.'

Later, when I pick Ben up from school, his teacher tells me he was sent to the school office for swearing. She's very apologetic about it.

'We know he doesn't mean it, but we have to send him to the office,' she says.

'Oh, I agree.'

'Poor Ben, he was shaking and white-faced when he got to the office and so the deputy was very gentle with him.'

Afterwards I say to Ben, 'Do you know why you swore at school?'

'No.'

'Maybe you were angry. Ben, if you get angry with someone, maybe with Mum or Dad, that's okay. But swearing is not okay. Ben, are you listening?'

'Yes,' he says. 'Mum, what's an angry face look like?'

I show Ben an angry face. Then he goes to get a big sheet of paper and starts drawing faces. At the top of the page he writes, 'What are you feeling today?' Each face has a different expression and the name of the feeling underneath. After he has drawn forty feelings, he brings the paper to me and shows me each face, asking me if he has ever felt that way. As well as the usual happy, sad, angry feelings, he has included dismal, smug, ambivalent and provocative.

'Have I ever felt provocative?' he asks.

'I would say so, yes.'

He's also included some made-up feelings.

'What's "statey" mean, Ben?'

'You know, when you say to me, "Don't get into a state, Ben."'

'Oh, I see. And what about "mongrateful"?'

'That's very grateful and happy. Have I ever felt mongrateful?'

'Maybe.'

'When did I feel mongrateful?'

'Well, when do you think?'

'I don't know.'

'Well,' I suggest, 'what about on your birthday when you got presents?'

'Yes. Now I'm going to make another face chart to take to Dad's house.'

Over the next few weeks, Ben spends a lot of time making face charts, standing in front of the mirror making faces and

talking about the different faces we make with different feelings. I think it's his way of telling us he is experiencing powerful emotions without having to express the emotions themselves
or understand where they come from. Often, it seems impossible for Ben to talk about or understand emotional things
directly, but at some level he grasps what's going on.

Ben loves to give me multiple-choice and true-or-false questions. One day, slipped in between two true-or-false questions
about school is an interesting multiple-choice question about
Frog (Ben), Toad (me) and Mole (Robert).

'Mum. Here's your next question. Toad, Frog and Mole all
lived together. But then, Mole moved out, leaving Frog and
Toad alone. Did Mole move out because: (a) Frog was sick; (b)
Mole wanted to go to the moon; (c) Mole was tired of Toad
nagging him about fixing up the house; or (d) Mole wanted a
house of his own?'

'Oh, let me see,' I say, trying not to laugh over option c. 'I
think, is it d?'

'Yes, correct.'

I love this question so much I ring up Olivia and tell her
about it. She laughs too.

'He's so clever,' she says.

'I never nagged!' I protest, half-serious.

'But I love the moon thing because of Robert and his astron-
omy,' says Olivia.

'I know. And the way he hints that Robert might have left
because he was "sick". Sort of like children who blame themselves for their parents separating.'

'Do you think he feels that? Feels that it's his fault or to do
with him? Because he's autistic?'

'No. And we've told him it isn't. But at some deeper, unconscious level, he might feel that.'

'He seems happy, though, doesn't he?' says Olivia.

'Yes, I think he's okay.'

I'm always reassuring people that Ben is happy. Few adults can handle the thought of an unhappy child, even though our own memories should tell us that children are often sad.

'Do you mind if I just walk up the stairs?' I ask the young man who now lives in the house that was once my own. 'Then I'll leave you in peace.'

'Yeah, okay.'

I walk to the top of the stairs, carpeted all the way to the edge now with proper underlay and glue, not the old way of half carpeting with tacks, leaving an edge of wood either side that had to be swept. I catch a glimpse of the bedroom doors. Only one door is open and I don't feel that I can look into any of the rooms, even though I'd like to see the bedroom I once shared with Pauline and Olivia. I know it will be changed: they will have recarpeted and repainted there as well, and because it is above the new sunroom I know there will no longer be climbing roses by the windows. I walk back down the stairs and to the front door.

'Thank you very much for letting me look around,' I say. 'Do you mind if I walk in the garden for a moment and take a few photos?'

'Nup, go ahead,' he replies, obviously glad to see the back of me, but still polite. As I walk to the front door, I catch a glimpse of a small area of wooden floor where the carpet has been taken up, perhaps because it was damaged or because a cupboard was once there. I recognise it immediately. It is the elaborate golden-coloured parquet floor we walked on every day. This floor, more than anything, shows the passing of time. It is scoured and damaged, a dull mustard colour, the wood shrunken so that the joins between each shape are filled with dirt. Because I am on my way out and thanking the young man, I see this, but don't really focus on it. Only later do I realise the impact it makes on me. Only later does this square of damaged parquet enter my dreams, throbbing like a living creature, calling me in the darkness.

I walk around the house to the back garden, and see that it, too, has changed. The grey stone wall, the garden beds, the funny stone post that held up one end of the washing line, the thirty-two cherry trees and the baby oak tree I grew from an acorn – all of these have vanished. Instead, there is a lawn and a few shrubs, a sensible, low-maintenance garden. It doesn't matter, though. Our real garden was the woods, the patch of trees and woodland plants that stretch from the boundary of the house to Keele Road on one side and the village green and Station Road on the other.

Before I go into the woods, I have one more place to visit. I walk down the path from our house to the 'hole in the wall', a place I would never go alone as a child, a place of fear. The hole in the wall is a break in the brick wall that runs one side of Keele Road. To get to school we would walk down to the hole in the wall, cross the road and then walk along the footpath until we reached the school. Once Olivia started school as well, my mother would simply walk us to the hole in the wall, help us cross the road and then leave Olivia and me to walk together. It was understood that we would hold hands and that Olivia would walk on the road side of the footpath because of my fear of traffic noise. In my memory, huge trucks would hurtle past us, throwing up a wave of dust and leaves, their roar amplified by the echoing wall. I'm smiling now as I stand in the hole in the wall, waiting for a truck. It doesn't seem like a very busy road now, but eventually a few cars drive past. I don't find them any noisier than cars on any other road.

Now is my time to visit the woods. This is what I have most wanted to do and I'm nervous that it won't live up to my expectations. I walk slowly, softly, along the muddy path, moving out of the sun and into dappled shade. I take ten, then another ten steps and I am here. The pale green light, the soft-edged shadows, the bird calls, the smell of rotting leaves and damp earth, the feathered touch of bracken on my ankles, the humid, slightly warm air – all of this enters my body and finds a deep and powerful echo. I find myself profoundly moved and can only stand here, drinking in every sensation. For the first time in my life, I feel I have discovered the landscape of home.

I walk in the woods for an hour. I see birds and a squirrel, no people. I see yellow and pink and blue flowers, stinging nettles and dock leaves, bushes with perfect places for a child to hide, moss and fungi on the roots of trees, the old brick hut that was the centre of our childhood games, the path to the village green that Pauline used when she took Olivia and me to feed the horses. As I see and smell and touch, words seem to float up through me. Long-forgotten words that belong to this place. Tree words: sycamore, maple, larch, beech and hawthorn. Plant words: buttercup, horsetail, celandine, dandelion, willowherb and wood sorrel. Bird names come to me as if called up by the sound of their songs: woodpecker, robin, house martin, wren, swallow, jackdaw, starling. I remember now the hedgehog we once left milk out for, the kingfishers we watched by the lakes, the white swans and their hisses, frog sounds on summer nights.

From the edge of the woods I can look over our garden and see the back of our house. Our bedroom windows catch the afternoon light, like square torches signalling to me. I remember the inside of our bedroom with its three single beds in a row, Pauline's escritoire and my mother's dollhouse. Already, the inside of the house as it is now has slipped from my mind. Instead I see images from the house of my childhood, long-held memories and also newly discovered ones, as if my body had stored them all these years and released them only when I entered the woods.

Eventually I leave the woods and walk across the village green, recognising a horse chestnut tree we used to collect conkers from, passing the single flashing beacon at the pedestrian crossing and ending up back at the bus stop.

It seems that I do have a sense of home after all. I just needed to revisit my childhood landscape to find it.

Bachelard writes that 'We do not have to be long in the woods to experience the ... impression of "going deeper and deeper" into a limitless world.' The forest may represent the mysterious unknown, the unconscious. Here was where my child self did her playing and dreaming, the precursors I suppose to my adult writing. This small patch of woods seemed vast to me then. As an adult, in another way, it is still vast, or rather deep. If the house is what Bachelard calls a 'geometry of echoes', then the woods, too, have their own echo, like a deep-sea radar.

We never leave behind our first intimate space, our large cradle of the house. We carry it with us to every other house we live in and every new space we encounter. It lives on in the imagination and in our night dreams.

As Mary Pershall describes it: 'Home has become for me, as I suspect it does for most migrants who stay away long enough, a kind of myth. I can still have the myth, shimmering inside my head, while I get on with life in my current home.'

*

'What are you doing, Mum?' asks Ben.

'I'm sorting through photos.' It is six months since I visited Keele and eighteen months since Robert and I separated. Ben goes back and forth quite happily every week. Ben and I still live in the same house. I wanted to move, but I didn't think it would be fair on Ben. He loves the garden here: the fish pond and waterfall, the grape vines, the fig tree, the secret passage behind the jasmine, the two eucalyptus trees standing taller than he can see, even the overgrown vegetable patch and waist-high weeds please him. He is nine now, almost the age I was when I left England. I want him to grow up with a sense of place, of belonging. To know what home means.

'Why are you sorting photos?' he asks.

'I'm choosing one of you to print on a mug for Dad for Christmas. As a present. What do you think? D'you think it's a good idea?'

'Yes.' After a pause, Ben says, 'Mum, families should have Christmas together. So I think you and me and Dad should have Christmas breakfast together.'

'That's a lovely idea, Ben. I'm sure we can do that.' I'm happy that he knows we're still a family, even though we live sepa-rately. 'Now, do you want to help choose a photo of yourself?'

'No, thank you.'

'Oh! Okay. Well, do you want to look at these photos of Keele? You know, the house I lived in when I was a kid.' I'm going to choose twelve photos to put on a calendar for my siblings.

'Yes,' says Ben, shuffling onto my lap. I cradle his back and rest my chin on the top of his head.

'Your house was bigger than mine,' he says.

'Yes, you're right. It was a big house. The garden was about the same size as ours here, though.'

'Did you have a trampoline?' he asks.

'No, we didn't.'

'Did you have a pond?'

'Not in our garden, no.'

'Did you have a scooter?'

'No. I'm not even sure they made scooters in those days.'

'What did you play, then?' asks Ben.

'Oh, we played in the woods. See these photos of the woods? That was our paradise.'

'What does paradise mean?'

'Oh. A paradise is a wonderful place. Somewhere really special.'

Ben thinks about this for a while.

'Mum, this is my paradise,' he says, waving his right hand, so that I'm not sure if he means the two of us, our house, the garden or just the world as he knows it, this moment, this place.

CARVING, FORGING, STEALING

*Writers are natural murderers. Their murderousness is a form of
sociopathy, fueled by resentment, scorn, glee and deep affection.*
—LYNN FREED

I CARVE OUT CHARACTERS. This one is abrupt and says
things no one wants to remember saying. That one is generous
and funny, and always arrives late. The man – Robert – has a
dry wit and talks little except to his son. The boy continually
asks questions. These characters are both people in my own
life and creations of my fingers on the computer keyboard.
When I write down a line one of my sisters has said, it is immediately transformed into something said by a character on my
page. Even if the words are accurately transcribed from life –
and how could they be, given I have only a normal faulty memory at my service? – they are changed by being written down,
by what I have written above and below them. If I were to read
these words to my sister, she might perhaps say, 'That isn't
what I said,' or 'I didn't mean that,' or 'You just made that up,
Rachel.'

I 'make things up' and then I believe them. I live my life
with dual vision. In my interactions with my family and friends
I am relating to the flesh and blood person but also to the character I have created on the page. Sometimes the two versions of

123

a person coincide and overlap; sometimes they clash and I look at Ben's father and think, 'What sort of a man are you?' because he is behaving in a way Robert would never behave.

'Rachel', too, is a character I have created. She is so close to me, I think, that anyone who knew me well would realise that she is a self-portrait. The self-portrait is partial, of course, because I know only some things about myself. But also, it is partial because the act of portrayal, of representation, seems to require some blurring and smudging, some cutting and sharpening. 'Rachel' is sometimes more naïve than her original, sometimes more shameful; she is weaker. And then sometimes she is wiser than I have ever been and steps back and watches where I would step in and damage. I thought I would be tempted to airbrush myself, to make me more attractive and better behaved than I feel I really am. But in fact, as I write, 'Rachel' quite happily enacts the worst of my behaviour as well as the best. The process of exposure, of revealing myself, seems much less important than the process of telling my story as honestly as I can. My fear that I would self-censor in order to protect myself and others has been unfounded. There is a deeper desire that is so powerful I seem able to sacrifice my own privacy.

A separate question is: how far am I prepared to sacrifice other people's privacy? What betrayals will I perpetrate on others?

When I was twenty and a university student, I fell in love with an English literature lecturer. I knew it was a cliché, even then, and that our affair would end badly for me. He knew that too, of course, and told me so. He was ten years my senior and a published author and I was in awe of him and infatuated. As predicted, things ended unhappily for me and I flew to London with a broken heart while the Poet (as I call him) continued his adulterous married life. For a few years I wrote him sad little letters full of literary devices and pretend pleasures. He occasionally wrote back letters of prevarication, ambivalence and restraint. Just the sight of the looping black letters of my name in his hand drove me to a frenzy of desire and hope, so that I would read the letters with frantic concentration, trying to suck some sustenance from his words. I was always disappointed. I suppose I wanted him to tell me that I was a person of value and loved or at least loveable, but of course he never said such a thing.

Eventually I got over my infatuation for the Poet. I grew older; life got busy; I met other men. Now and again, the Poet and I would exchange notes or cards and he always sent me copies of his books. One day, eight years after we parted, I received the Poet's new novel in the post. On the title page, in that same looping hand, was written: 'To Rachel, at last, with love and gratitude, this house of ghosts and memories'. To say that I was a character in that novel would be completely untrue. But still, I was there. I recognised myself. There was a woman who loved a man without return. That woman was flawed in a particular way and I recognised that flaw. She dreamed a dream that eight years ago was my dream, one I had retold the Poet. In this novel, the woman and the man write letters to each other. The man's letters form part of the novel and these letters I recognised also, because they were only slightly changed versions of those disappointing letters I had received from the Poet in London. I suppose the Poet kept photocopies of all the letters he wrote. The letters are replies to the woman's letters, which the reader never gets to read but which are shaped in our minds by the nature of her ex-lover's replies.

It's a common enough story. Writers use real life as their

material. They write down interesting conversations and dreams. They go back to their own work – old poems, draft stories, letters to friends – and use the bits they like for their current work. The Poet had never pretended to be a person of outstanding integrity – after all, I got to know him while he cheated on his wife. He had warned me that he would do me no good. Still, in spite of knowing all this, I admit I was shocked and enraged when I read that novel. I wrote him a furious letter, telling him he had betrayed my trust. (Yes, a letter – it seems I never learn from my mistakes.) But mostly I felt shamed, and this was what stayed with me after the anger and sense of betrayal abated. The shame of the dream. The shame of unrequited love. Most of all, I felt shame that words written to me by a man I loved were in fact not private, not personal, not a gift to me, but part of a novel.

I did think of revenge. Yes, indeed, I had many fantasies of writing my own story, outing the Poet for adultery and dream stealing! But revenge, of course, doesn't heal shaming – that is something we have to deal with internally.

This happened a long time ago now and so it is like thinking of something that happened to someone else, not me. Now, I realise that my reactions were coloured by many other things, one of which was my sense that the Poet had stolen my voice. When I met the Poet I was young and hopeful and wanted to be a writer. But I was insecure and somehow ashamed of my desire to write; I felt that I might have no talent. Perhaps I fell for him because he was what I wanted to become. When he rejected me, I managed to translate that into my own rejection of the dream of becoming a writer. This wasn't necessarily a conscious decision. It related in some way to a feeling that my sexual self had been damaged by our relationship. When he replied to my first letter from London saying, 'Your letter is a little self-conscious.

You probably will be a writer after all,' I felt terribly humiliated. Deep within me I began to feel that I would never, could never, be a writer.

The Poet, of course, is not to blame for my insecurities as a young woman. In fact, he is not to blame for anything in this story. But I think of it now because I am at risk of doing to others what I once experienced as so painful. In effect to represent others is to steal their story. This can have profound consequences.

Before my son reached the age of four, I had breached his privacy many times. I continue to do this. It is part of living with disability. You are asked to tell your story to strangers all the time. What you are asked to tell as a parent is a particular type of story. The scaffolding for the story is provided by the context and the professional you are talking to. When Ben was being diagnosed, I spent hours answering questions put to me by a developmental paediatrician, a psychologist and a speech pathologist. The paediatrician asked about developmental milestones and physical health. The psychologist was interested in play and relationships. The speech pathologist focused on language. All these separate stories came together only in me. I kept trying to return to Ben as a whole person, but then I would get derailed into details, like the way he mixed up pronouns or what he did in noisy places. At the end of the process, the paediatrician wrote a five-page report on Ben, indicating which of the criteria he met for a diagnosis of autism and why. Reading it was a strange experience. It was true but untrue. It seemed to be less a story about Ben than about a boy who failed to do certain things that his mother and these professionals expected him to do. The woman in the story – that is, me – was also strange. The report was full of phrases like, 'The mother reports that ...' and 'According to the mother ...' It was only on reading the report that I realised the extent to which I act as translator and mediator between Ben and the rest of the world. Of course, all parents do this with young children, but I realised then the power of that role when your child has a disability.

This was only the start of my form filling and question answering. Now, I am quite used to completing a long and detailed form before I can enrol Ben in any activity or have any new person work with him. I have completed sensory profile questionnaires, school disability funding applications, forms for respite, for special activities, for parent training funds, for adaptive technology, for everything really, even things that we turn out to be ineligible for or unable to use. I have briefed psychologists, speech pathologists, occupational therapists, therapy assistants, schoolteachers, education assistants, sports instructors, swimming teachers, hairdressers, dentists, neighbours and childcare providers. Every time I talk about Ben, I am rehearsing his life story, choosing which things I need to say and which I leave out. I am exposing his challenges, anxieties and preoccupations to a stranger who will work with him for a while, but who usually moves on within less than a year. And each person takes notes. They have a file on Ben at the school, at the Disability Services local and head offices, the local council, the non-government agency that is supposed to provide services to the school, the respite service we never use, the childcare service he is too old to use, the doctor's surgery, the hospital, and the offices of all our private therapists and all the researchers who have asked us to participate in autism research.

The further I went in my career as a medical subject (oh yes, 'the mother' is a subject too), the more I realised that the process of completing forms and answering questions resulted in a series of stories about Ben (and me) that had the potential to define him. The purpose of giving information to professionals, schools and community groups is to help them work more effectively with your child. That is totally benign. But how benign is it that little pieces of Ben's life are lying around this whole city, out of our control, never retrievable?

The story of the dream-stealing Poet has a postscript. A few years ago a friend told me that she was browsing on the website of a literary archive when she came across the Poet's name. He had sold his manuscripts and letters to this archive.

'Did you know he sold his letters to you?' she asked.

'How do you know?' I wondered.

'Your name's there, Rachel, on the website.'

'But I have his letters.'

'But he copied them, didn't he?'

'Oh. So people can read the letters?' This was a silly question, of course, because anyone could read the letters in the novel.

'No, Rachel.' My friend gave her wasn't-I-right-after-all sort of smile. 'Some of the folios are closed until after the author's death. His letters to you are in one of those.'

'Until after *his* death?'

'Yes, that's right. Planning to outlive him, are you?'

One of the things about autism is that researchers love it. This is good because it means there is lots of research going on. (Not that most of it actually helps autistic people live a fuller life.) Researchers, of course, need subjects and in a small city and country that means that parents of autistic children get lots of enquiries about whether they might participate in research. At first I was keen because I felt that it was a responsible thing to do and that more information might help Ben in some way. So I filled out sleep diaries and food diaries and did telephone interviews and kept a record of the number of hours of direct intervention Ben received and any results I could observe. And I took Ben for IQ and behavioural tests – made him sit in small square rooms with me while strangers asked him odd questions.

The event that ended our research participation involved three tests all rolled into one: an EEG, a blood test and a gut-permeability test. He was only four years old and I wasn't sure how he would handle this, but I felt it was worth the risk because we would be given the results. Many autistic children suffer from epilepsy and an EEG can give some warning of epilepsy in advance. The gut-permeability test also provides some indication of food intolerances and so, again, I thought that would be useful information. I suppose it was useful: it showed that Ben's gut seemed normal and that his EEG included some abnormalities but none that especially indicated epilepsy. Still, that information came at some cost to Ben.

It was a Friday. In the morning, Ben had to fast and could drink only water. That wasn't too hard. We had to put anaesthetic cream on the inside of his elbows so that he wouldn't feel any pain when they took blood. We used transparent bandaids ('Like little windows,' I said) to keep the cream on. Ben really hated those bandaids and kept trying to rip them off and crying when I wouldn't let him. I took him across the road to the park and he sat crying on the slide, saying, 'Please take off windows.' An hour later we drove to the children's hospital and entered the neurological suite. This was like any other hospital room except for a few dog-eared children's posters on the walls and some dusty toys in a basket in the waiting room.

'Not exactly welcoming, is it?' murmured Robert.

'Don't like here,' proclaimed Ben.

In order to do the gut-permeability test, Ben needed to drink a whole cup full of sugary liquid. When they took blood in an hour's time, they would then test how much of the starch had leaked into the bloodstream. At the same time, Ben had to drink a small dose of cough mixture. For the EEG, he had to be sedated and the least harmful way to sedate a child in terms of research protocol was deemed to be cough mixture. The only problem was, Ben refused to drink either of these mixtures. So I held him down while Robert and the nurse forced the cough mixture down his throat with a syringe and held his mouth closed until he swallowed. That experience made him even less interested in drinking the sugar liquid. According to the nurse, I was to rock Ben to sleep while making sure he drank the liquid. I did my best. I started with reading him books and singing lullabies. We dimmed the lights and I told him to lie down and sleep. It was eleven in the morning; Ben didn't feel sleepy and he certainly couldn't relax in a strange environment, with windows on his elbows and thick fluids being forced down his throat. After some time, the nurse said she would use their back-up sedation method – something squirted up his nose. This caused Ben to scream and run to the door, banging on it to be let out. Eventually he did start to tire, I think partly because he was so scared and upset he had worn himself out. He lay on my lap, arms around my waist, while I recited the times tables to him because I knew that would be the most reassuring thing I could say. The nurse looked at me with slight horror when I changed from 'twinkle twinkle' to 'two times two'. Perhaps she thought I'd lost it. I remember sitting there, muddling up six times seven with six times eight and just carrying on reciting the wrong numbers anyhow. And finally he gave up the struggle and slept.

'He's a fighter,' remarked Robert, patting my back for reassurance.

We laid him on a hard bed and the EEG technician came in and placed electrodes all over his skull before hooking him up to the machine. Then we were asked to leave so that our voices didn't influence the results. We sat with our coffees in the hospital café and did what Robert and I always do at such times, probably what most people do – we told each other what a brave child we had and made black jokes at our own expense.

An hour later, the EEG was finished and the final tasks were to take blood and then remove all the electrodes from Ben's head.

'We'll take the blood now,' said the nurse, 'because he's still out to it.'

'He'll wake though, won't he?' asked Robert.

'Oh no, they never wake.'

Robert and I exchanged a glance. I moved to the head of the bed and Robert stood on one side. As soon as she inserted the needle, Ben woke and started struggling and screaming. Robert and the EEG technician held him down, and the nurse took the blood all from one arm – three vials full – while I held Ben's face in my hands, placing my own very close, and counted with him. Finally the electrodes came off his head and we could go home.

'He'll be very groggy all day,' warned the nurse. 'He'll probably drop back to sleep in the car or later at home. They always have another nap after sedation.'

Ben wanted to walk to the car park, but his legs kept wobbling, so he allowed Robert to carry him. He didn't sleep in the car – he wanted to eat instead. I put videos of *Bananas in Pyjamas* on for him in the afternoon and he sat down with his legs splayed like a yoga master and watched them for two hours. He didn't sleep until his normal bedtime.

'Just rock him to sleep. They never wake with the bloods. They always sleep after sedation,' I quoted to Robert in a cruel imitation of the nurse that night.

'Like I say,' said Robert, 'he doesn't give up easily.'

'He doesn't forget, either,' I suggested. And I was right. Regularly, for the next year or so, Ben would refer to that event and ask me why I was so mean, making him wear windows on his elbows and holding him down while the nurse took blood for over 120 counts. He wasn't angry with me or let down so much as mystified and determined to remind me that it wasn't a good experience. He made me promise that I would never do that to him again. It was three years before he would agree to wear another bandaid.

Privacy is about control. Control over our own body, space and possessions and control over information about ourselves. In *Secrets*, Sissela Bok defines privacy as 'the condition of being protected from unwanted access by others'. She says: 'Claims to privacy are claims to control access to what one takes – however grandiosely – to be one's personal domain.' Most people see their own bodies, their possessions and their creations as part of their personal domain. She points out, however, that some parents see their children as part of their domain as well. I think she would suggest that these parents are being grandiose, because a child is likely to consider him or herself the appropriate person to determine the access others may have to his or her own space and self.

Bok points out that 'unwarranted access' by others can include not only the revelation of personal matters but also simple observation by others. For example, we may feel our privacy is invaded if we discover that we are under surveillance. In a similar way, writing about someone without revealing any secrets or anything negative may still violate a person's privacy. Bok argues in favour of 'partial individual control over the degree of secrecy or openness about personal matters'. Without such partial control, she says, it would be impossible to 'preserve the indispensable respect for identity' that we should all be able to claim. Here Bok is arguing that privacy and identity are closely interwoven.

This is really about power: 'Control over secrecy and openness gives power.' When you write autobiographically about yourself and others, you are giving yourself some form of authority in relation to the truth of your tale. Others, including readers, may question that authority, may resist the exercise of your power.

I started writing about my life as a parent in 2005 and never stopped.

'What are you writing?' my friends and family would ask me occasionally.

'Just about my life,' I would reply, before changing the subject. No one ever said, 'Are you going to publish it?' or 'Am I in it?' I'm not sure if this indicates the lack of seriousness with which others viewed my writing or just their fine sense of discretion and restraint.

The first time people started to consider that this work would be published was when I enrolled in a doctorate. Even then, it wasn't something I really focused on until I had to gain approval from the university's Human Research Ethics Committee. I don't think of myself as doing research involving humans. I think of my research as reading books. But because I am writing about my own life and family, including my son, the university considered this research to involve 'human participants'. Should I be seeking informed consent from my family to write about them? Will I cause any harm to them through my research? How can I protect my family from the results of my research? Should Robert act as an advocate for my son and approve my work for publication? These are the sorts of questions that I had to ask myself.

They are confronting questions because I think of myself as my son's advocate. I believe that I am the one person standing between him and a cruel, exploitative world. I don't want to see myself in the role of exploiter, even though many people might consider I am exploiting him by writing about him.

In a sense, the ethics committee has required me to rethink the ethics of my writing. I have had to compare my own project with other forms of research, such as medical research, ethnography and psychology. There is a strange irony in this because I feel as though I am writing partly to question some of the theories resulting from medical and psychological research on autism.

Because the issue troubled me, I talked to several friends about it. In every case, their response was to say that because my motives are pure, I shouldn't have to worry about this.

'You're not writing a kiss-and-tell exposé of a famous exhusband, are you?' said one friend.

'I don't even have an ex-husband,' said I.

'Not yet, anyhow,' she replied (once again proving herself more astute than I was).

After a few of these conversations, I realised what was angering and worrying me about all of this. It wasn't that I was being treated as a potentially exploitative parent or being judged to have sinister motives for writing about my family. No, the thing that was bugging me was: this was my story and I wanted to write it my way, without censorship. I recognised that all scholarship and creative writing involves negotiating ideas of 'truth'.

I also recognised that I would have to compromise in order to protect my son and that protecting my son was very important to me – but still, I wanted to be free to write whatever I felt and thought. On the one hand, I'm a little horrified at my own desire to write my life my way. On the other hand, I'm rather amazed and impressed that after forty years of not saying what I want, I'm finally determined to. I see that I have a kind of ruthlessness that is troubling and reassuring at the same time.

It's probably good that the ethics committee didn't know about the ruthlessness!

Questions of privacy and the ownership of one's own story are complicated, of course, by contemporary views of the self. It makes sense to talk about protecting a boy's privacy from his mother's desire to violate it if we think of identity as involving a discrete, autonomous self. But contemporary models of identity are much more fluid, reflecting the idea of the self-in-process rather than a single stable identity. The fixed humanist self may be the model of identity most of us use in our daily lives and in institutions such as the law, but it isn't going to be very useful in contemporary life writing, which enacts and represents more fluid notions. In his book *How Our Lives Become Stories*, Paul John Eakin suggests that 'if our identities and lives are more entangled with those of others than we tend to acknowledge ... then existing models of privacy, personhood, and ethics may have to be revised.'

To me, the bond between mother and child seems the closest relationship one could ever write about. My own body was my son's first home. In everyday life we may think of our body as our most tangible and permanent boundary but in fact the body, too, is permeable and fragmented. Sidonie Smith suggests that a history of the body is inscribed in all women's autobiography in one way or another. For a mother, writing about your child is, in one sense, writing the history of your body.

I think it must be true that I don't learn from my mistakes because my lover M is also a poet. Even though we live in different cities, we don't write each other letters. Sometimes, though, we will send a brief email – the sort you might send to any friend. He sends me poems too and sometimes the inspiration for these poems is something I have said or done. But I have no fears from this poet. After forty it's much harder to feel betrayed or shamed by people! Last time I saw him, I asked him if he minded my putting him in my book under a different name. He smiled in that way that crinkles his eyes and stretches his lips thin and said, 'Of course not.'

Other people won't feel the same. They will be angry and hurt that I have written about them. Changing names won't change their feelings. They will feel this even if I make it clear that what I have written is not 'the truth' but only 'my truth'. Even if I call my work fiction, I may still hurt others. Lynn Freed says that writers, when faced with a choice between truth and decency, will always choose truth. She describes this as a form of 'pathological ruthlessness':

> It involves not only the obvious indecencies, the revelation
> of bathroom habits and petty adulteries, but, more than
> this, the revelation, through the story, through the charac-
> ters in the story, of the human condition itself – its sadness,
> its absurdity, its loneliness, its familiarity. Is there a safe
> and decent way to accomplish this? I don't think so. If it is
> done right, someone will be hurt.

I have no idea how to navigate my way through this issue. I thought at first that perhaps if it was my own bathroom habits and petty adulteries that I revealed then this would be a safe and decent way to write autobiography. But it isn't that simple. My life is so linked to others that they are implicated too.

The story of the dream-stealing Poet has another postscript. When I was writing this essay, I needed to look in the Poet's novel to check what it was he had written inside. In my mind I thought it was something a bit pretentious and impersonal. When I read his words I was surprised: they seemed personal, generous and not at all pretentious. I hadn't remembered that he had sent me 'love and gratitude'. The love part I understand. Even though at twenty-one I was quite sure he didn't love me, I have since realised the many and varied forms that love can take. But gratitude is more complex. What had he to thank me for, I wonder?

I then flicked through the novel, something I hadn't done for many years. I quickly found the page with 'my' dream. Another surprise: it wasn't an exact reproduction of my dream after all. It was close; two of the images were from my dream, but the sequence wasn't exactly the same. I know this because I kept a dream diary in my twenties. I lost the diary ages ago, but found it again in a box of papers (in company with many earwigs and spiders) when I last moved house.

Years too late, I feel great compassion for the Poet, and indeed for my then self.

Like me, Ben is very interested in stories. Like me, he gets muddled about versions of truth, self and reality.

'Mum, what do *real* unicorns look like?' he will ask. Or, 'Is this a fiction or non-fiction story?' I often find it quite difficult to answer because his stories are both true and make-believe at once. To create his stories he mixes the plots from books we have read together with events from his life. For example, he will take the basic structure of Beatrix Potter's *The Story of a Fierce Bad Rabbit*, change the rabbits to a frog and a toad and then elaborate along the lines of bad and good things he does at home and what happens to the good frog and bad toad. The protagonist of most of Ben's stories is Frog, his alter ego. It seems that Ben, too, is writing his autobiography. But – as he often says when I try to move him from one subject to another – 'that's another story'.

PUMPKIN SCONES

School's a weird thing. I'm not sure it works.—JOHNNY DEPP

IT'S LOUD — INCREDIBLY, horribly loud. And it's dark, with lots of flashing coloured lights. I'm sitting alone on a wooden bench at one side of the hall, forcing a stiff smile while tears roll down my cheeks. The music bounces and distorts against the brick walls and my head thuds in time with the flashing lights. But that's not why I'm crying alone in the dark. I'm crying because I'm watching Ben at his first school disco. Even in this half-light I can pick him out from the hundred or so other children here, partly because he is the only child dancing on his own and partly because of the nature of his movements. His 'dancing' is a kind of jumping, interspersed with a few sideways steps every now and then, his arms bent at the elbow, his hands pointing upwards. It's not that his movements are really weird; they're just slightly strange. But if I scan the hall, my eye immediately finds him because of that stiff-gaited body language, seemingly unique to Ben.

'Mum, there's a senior disco at school. Shall I go?' he'd asked me a few weeks earlier.

'What do you think? Would you like to?'

'I don't know. What happens at a disco?'

'I'm not entirely sure, Ben. But I think there is music and

kids dance and hang out together.' The last time I went to a disco was in the days of John Travolta and *Saturday Night Fever*.

'Will it be noisy?' asked Ben.

'Yes, the music will be loud.'

'Will I like it?'

'I don't know. Why not give it a try?'

I was surprised that Ben was even considering going to the disco. Apart from the noise and the fact he'd never been to one before, he's only been at this school a few months and so he doesn't really know many kids and certainly doesn't have mates to hang out with at a social event. He decided to go, though, and took some care with his clothes, wearing jeans, a skull T-shirt that I said would look cool and a glow-in-the-dark shark's tooth on a leather cord. He was very anxious before-hand but didn't back out.

When I think about the courage it took Ben to come to this disco, knowing it would be loud and being new to the school, I am so proud of him. And yet, for the last hour, he has been on his own doing his weird dance and I feel choked with grief for him as well. Not one child has come up to him. Not one teacher has introduced him to a group of other children. (Even at this school, inclusion is never total.) The girls group together, talking and laughing and sometimes dancing. The boys hang in smaller groups at the edges of the hall, occasionally showing off their break-dance steps, but mainly sipping cans of soft drink and just wandering around.

Ben stops dancing and comes over to me. 'I'm having a good time, Mum,' he says in a way that makes me think he knows I've been watching him. He can't see my tears because it's too dark, but I put on a bigger smile and say, 'That's great, Ben. Would you like a drink or some food? They're selling crisps and lollies.'

'Yes, please.' We go up to the counter together, because he doesn't feel confident to go on his own. He buys a small bag of crisps and a bottle of water. I think he's the only kid in the whole room who chooses water over soft drink.

'Why don't you sit with me and have your snack now?' I suggest.

'Okay, Mum, just for a bit. Because I'm enjoying myself,' he says pointedly.

'That's great. So you like discos. Actually, Ben, I've got a headache from the loud music, so I wouldn't mind leaving a bit early, if that's okay with you.' I say this not because it's true (which it is) but because I can tell Ben is quite exhausted from the last hour and I'm not sure that he'll last another half hour without getting distressed. I think if I provide the excuse, it will be easier for him to leave early.

'I'm going to dance, Mum,' he says and leaves me with the rest of the water. Back he goes, into an open space, doing his dance, this time watching me watching him. On goes my false smile. Then I turn my head, so that I'm watching other children instead – the poor kid should have a break from his anxious mum! Are they enjoying themselves, I wonder? There's lots of shrieking and excitement.

What sort of a world is it, I wonder, that an occasion like this counts as a great social event? When an assault on the senses is considered fun? When not being able to communicate with others is something to look forward to? If this is the 'normal' neurotypical world, please let me off!

Ben is suddenly back with me, taking the water bottle for a drink. He looks both weary and wired.

'My headache is worse. Would you be ready to go now, Ben?' I ask.

'Okay,' he says and we walk out the door. The cool, quiet

night is like a soft cloth on my face. As we walk to the car, we pass a girl on her way to the toilet.

'Hi, Brianna,' says Ben. 'Did you enjoy the disco?'

'Yes, but I'm not leaving yet.'

'Have a good time,' says Ben.

When we get to the car, I say, 'Well, how was your first school disco?'

'It was good.'

'What was the best part?' I ask. Ben pauses for a bit and then says, 'Talking to Brianna was the best part.'

Great, I think to myself, I went through all that pain and the best part wasn't even anything to do with the disco!

'I'm really proud of you for going, Ben.'

'Mum, what's happening on the weekend?' asks Ben.

He's already moving on and we haven't even made it home yet. I, however, will be haunted by the disco for several weeks. In fact, I can't get the vision of watching Ben out of my mind until I tell Penny about it. I don't realise quite why it's so painful for me until she says, 'You were reliving your own school days, perhaps?' I think she is right. Seeing Ben all on his own at a social event made me sad for him and for me as his mother, but it also triggered memories of my own loneliness at school: the sensory overload, the paralysing shyness, my inability to fit in.

It is autumn and I am four years old. I have been deserted, cast out without explanation. A feeling possesses me, as if a balloon were being blown up in my chest. It keeps getting larger and it presses upon me. I have never felt this way before. I don't understand what it is and why it is happening. Why no one can see that this is happening and why they don't comfort me. It has been torn from me – the familiar daily routine, looking after

Olivia, playing together in our room, in the garden, helping Mother in the kitchen, living our normal life.

First there is the walk. Into the hole in the wall, along the road with its hurtling lorries and slashing cars, shoulders hunched against the noise, eyes down, fastening on each leaf on the footpath, their different shapes a frail barrier against what is about to come. Then the noise of dozens of children in the playground, like bees swarming around a centre that I never grasp. Sitting in the classroom, in an agony of anxiety in case I am asked a question and I have to speak in front of the class.

This is to happen every day, I discover. It is not just once or twice, but forever. Only weekends are different; then we can go back to normal. But it is not the same, because I can't forget that on Monday it will all start again. I don't understand why this is happening to me. It is so bad that I realise I must have been very wicked. No one from my family wants to be with me any more. I have to be with the nameless, faceless, wild children in the nursery-school room.

I try to be very good. I have always tried to be good, but now I try even harder. Perhaps if I help Mother more and keep Olivia quiet and busy so she can go into her study, perhaps then I will be so useful that Mother will want me to stay at home again. I try not to cry on the walk. I don't ask again if I can stay home. When I am asked if I had a good time at nursery school, I always say 'yes' now because that is the correct answer. I still look at the floor all the time, but I listen now and learn the names of the children, so that I can answer Mother's questions on the way home.

It doesn't get easier, but I learn ways to cope. Fantasy is one way. Making myself very small and still is another. The best way, though, is reading. There are books at nursery school and I am one of the few children who like them; the others just flip through the pages looking at the pictures and then run off to play together. Quite often, we sit four children at a table and are taught how to read. Because I can already read, I always finish my book before the others and have to sit and wait. I soon learn to read the books of the other children at the table; reading sideways and upside down is no different from reading right way up. Now I have four stories to keep me company during the day.

In spite of my tears at the disco, I'm actually thrilled with Ben's new school and the way he has settled in. I thought maybe it would take him six months before he felt comfortable there but in fact it took only a few weeks. Although it is just two kilometres down the road from his old school and both are state schools, the difference is huge. His old school had only one hundred and fifty children, small classes, old buildings, few extra resources and teachers who were mainly very dedicated but not always highly skilled. This new school has four hundred students, large class sizes, a lot more resources, some very skilled teachers and an excellent leadership team. It also has a resource room for children with special needs: Room 5, Ben's home away from home. Ben spends about half of each day in Room 5 with a modified curriculum and extra support staff. The rest of the day he spends doing the same work and activities as his peers in a regular classroom.

Even though Ben spends half his time in Room 5, in some ways he is more integrated in this new school than at the old one. For example, he is now a member of the school hockey team and plays in interschool competitions. It's true he tends to shoot 'own goals' but the other team members tease him only a little about this. Similarly, he joins in the music lessons, whereas at his previous school he skipped music because the teacher felt it was too noisy for him. At this school they are working with Ben to help him tolerate more noise and develop strategies to handle overstimulation.

Both schools have access to the same level of funding from the state government to work with Ben, but the way they use these funds is very different. Ben was happy at his old school and I felt it was a perfect place for him when he was younger. The small size and nurturing approach seemed ideal. As he got older, though, his needs changed and I felt the school no longer offered him an adequate education.

When I first thought about schooling for Ben, I was sure that I wanted him to be in a mainstream class in a mainstream school and that he would do well if he just had some additional one-to-one support. While I could see that some students needed a segregated environment, I favoured full inclusion for Ben. Over time, I have become a little more flexible in my thinking. I now think that integrating children with disabilities requires accomodations that go beyond simply adding on a part-time education assistant and putting up a few visual sched-ules. A separate environment within a school, like Room 5, can actually be more inclusive than just dropping the child into the mainstream setting and telling him to cope. But I would never have considered this a good option when Ben was four and I was looking at local schools. At that stage, I was desperate for Ben to 'fit in'. Seven years ago, I was still afraid of school.

The row of bags on hooks outside the Blue Room flips me into a child's body. I feel, once again, the sensation of an empty lift falling inside my chest. My steps get smaller, my shoulders tighter, I feel myself swallow.

'Where are we going?' asks Ben and I am adult again, taking my son to the school to enrol for kindergarten next year.

'We're going to the Red Room. Can you see it?'

'Here it is!' he announces, smiling.

I've decided to play this one low-key. When we left home I told Ben we were going to the local shops – which he likes – but that first I had to drop into the school. I haven't said that this will be where he goes to kindergarten next year.

In the Red Room is Mrs W, the teacher, and two other parents with their children, one boy, one girl. There are several boxes of educational toys, including a box full of coloured calculators.

'Ben, this is Mrs W.'

'Hello, Mrs W,' says Ben.

Mrs W knows Ben is autistic but hasn't met him before. She gives me three (long) forms to complete and encourages Ben to play with the toys. I sit on a child's chair at a child's table with my forms. The little girl is taking out each of the calculators and laying them on the floor in a row. Ben goes up to her and says 'hello' but she ignores him. He wanders off to read an alphabet animal poster. The mother of the boy is having trouble understanding the form. I think she's Chinese. Mrs W is having trouble understanding her trouble. The boy calls to his mother in their language but she doesn't respond and so he starts to smash the toy he's been playing with. Things get a little out of hand, and the girl – all thirty-odd calculators lined up on the floor now – starts to whinge. Ben watches and listens and then comes up to me.

'What are they doing?' he asks. I don't answer, because I'm wondering why the other two children are behaving like this and why Ben isn't lining up the calculators and counting them himself. I finish my forms very quickly (so much recent experience!) and then hand them to Mrs W. After a brief chat we leave.

'Goodbye, Mrs W,' says Ben, without any prompting.

We skip out of the room, a huge grin on my face. I'm so proud of him!

Then we see a boy who looks about nine years old running across the playground. The school principal is following him, doing a fast march like in the Olympic walking competition and calling out, 'Shane, this is ridiculous, Shane, you have a choice.'

'What are they doing?'

'I'm not sure, Ben. I think the teacher is following the boy to help him.'

For some reason, I find the sight of the principal chasing a little boy reassuring. It suggests that he errs on the side of kind rather than strict.

'I'll be coming here next year,' says Ben matter-of-factly.

'Yes, that will be fun, won't it?' I say, surprised that he's worked it out already. 'You'll enjoy kindy, especially with Mrs W.' Aware of my own hypocrisy as I speak, but saying it anyhow, wanting desperately to believe it.

By the time February comes around, I discover that the school principal has changed and that the kindergarten class will be held in a new venue with a different teacher. I try to take this information in my stride, but it makes me uneasy.

The week before school starts, Ben and I go to visit the new teacher and Ben's part-time education assistant. We've had a tough week. Yesterday saw us in a local café, Ben throwing himself on the floor screaming, 'Don't put pepper on my chips,' while I pretended not to notice the dagger-looks from other patrons. The day before we'd had an altercation with the mother of a two-year-old whom Ben had pushed off a swing. And this morning, I found myself yelling at Ben because he wakes up at five and makes lots of noise. ('Of course he does,' says Robert, 'he's a child.' I don't bother explaining that it wasn't the noise as such; it was the thirty-minute recitation of the times tables that got to me.) Now we're finally walking to school, Ben seems quite calm and relaxed. I, however, am worried about: the fact that Ben's education assistant will only be at school two of the four mornings; how Ben will cope with being left with strangers; whether he will be aggressive with other children; how he'll go with toileting; whether he will try to run away; how he will cope with a noisy environment; how he'll manage with the craft activities; and how understanding and skilled the staff will be.

'Here we are, Ben, you can knock at the door,' I suggest.

'I don't want to.'

I knock at the door and we walk into a small, hot room that smells just a little of toilets. It's a mess in here. There are things everywhere and we have to step over rolls of cardboard and boxes of textas and scissors just to get into the room. Two women turn and smile at us and suddenly I think, it'll be fine. The teacher is in her forties; the education assistant is older. They are both welcoming to me and quiet and gentle with Ben. He wanders around the room looking out for interesting objects as I talk to Mrs D. He soon finds a chart with numbers on it and hunkers down for a good stare. The assistant, Mrs R, goes to sit near him, says hello, and waits for him to respond to her. Immediately, I know that she understands how to relate to children with autism. As I talk with the teacher, I see that Ben has said a few things to Mrs R without looking at her or seeming to pay her any attention. She replies to him and he laughs and races across the room to wrap his arms around my legs. Mrs D and Mrs R smile at me. I can see they are kindly and caring women. They ask sensible questions; they accept the notes on Ben I have written and promise to read them tonight;

they stress that I am welcome to stay with Ben in the classroom as long as I like and that they will consult with me about Ben regularly. A great weight seems to drop from me.

Just as we are about to leave, the new principal enters the room. He is young, very tall and good looking. And he has charisma. I can't see him having to do the Olympic walk across the playground; no child would dare to run away from him. We talk for five minutes and already I feel that he is a warm man and an efficient principal.

As we walk back home, I say to Ben, 'Well, they seemed like lovely people, didn't they? I think you'll enjoy going there next week.'

Ben asks, 'Will the chart with numbers from one to one hundred be there?'

'Oh yes.'

'We can look at that,' he says, satisfied.

I'm a bit puzzled by the 'we'. Has he used it by accident, meaning I? Or does it refer to him and the other children? Or does he mean what he usually does when he says we – him and me? It strikes me that I have never sat down and explained to Ben that children go to school without their parents. It's not like some therapy sessions where I stay and am involved. Surely he would know this? But I'm actually not sure that he does. I decide to talk about it over the weekend when we read some of our books about starting school. I try not to think about Ben's thirty-minute crying sessions whenever I left him at day care last year.

That night, I tell Robert about our visit to the school and try to reassure him. He's more anxious than I am.

'I can't believe Ben's really going to start school. He doesn't seem old enough,' he says.

'I know.'

'How will he cope without us, four mornings a week?' Robert wonders.

'He'll be okay,' I say. 'I expect all parents worry in just the same way before their kids start school.' I don't mention my concern that Ben might think I'll be with him in school. And I don't say what I really think: that starting school is a milestone for parents as well as for children, that it is a time for celebration and pride as well as anxiety and a little sadness. For a parent of a child with a developmental disability, transitions are always hard and the celebration tends to get swamped by fear and grief – you see how your child is different, left far behind the other children. I don't say this because, already, I have started to censor what I say to Robert. Already, I sense I need to protect him. At the time, I'm not even aware I am doing this; I don't recognise that I have passed another milestone.

I remember very little about my own schooling, beyond those early memories of nursery school. Olivia, two years younger than I, can tell me the names of my teachers from primary school and my best friends.

'I had friends at school in Keele, then?' I ask her.

'Of course you did. Well, you had three good friends,' she replies. 'But you remember primary school in Perth, don't you? You were ten years old then.'

I pretend to her that I remember a bit more, and I do have a few pictures in my mind: my first Australian athletics carnival and the shame of coming last in everything; not knowing how to dive into the school swimming pool; not understanding 'new maths'; the bizarre names of explorers I had never heard of like 'Burke-en-Wills' and Vlamingh; being teased with the chant 'brum brum' because of the way I said words like broom

151

and room. Of course I was an outsider: I spoke funny and was hopeless at sport.

High school was a little easier. By then, I'd learned to mimic fitting in a bit better and was slightly less terrified of all the other kids. Some of the other girls befriended me and tried (unsuccessfully) to make me seem less obviously uncool. Still, I seem to have wiped most of my schooling from my memory. Not long ago, I started working with a new colleague on a project. Some months into our work, he asked, 'Are you going to the reunion?'

'Sorry?' I said, wondering what on earth he was talking about.

'You know, our thirtieth school reunion. Did you get the email about it?'

'Um ... no, I didn't.'

'I'll forward it on.'

I gathered from this that my colleague and I had been at high school together. I rang Laura, the one school friend I have kept up with, and asked her about this colleague. 'Was he really in our year?'

'Of course he was! You're not saying you don't remember him? Rachel, he sat next to you in every English lesson during year twelve!'

'Oh,' I said. 'He looked a bit familiar, but I thought it was just seeing him at work.'

'Rachel, I can't believe you don't remember. Has he changed that much?'

I checked out the photographs that were by now posted online. In fact, my colleague hadn't changed one bit – he seems to have aged without changing at all. I looked at the other faces – rows of seventeen-year-olds with strange late-'70s haircuts, mine the worst of all. About ten of the faces rang a bell; it seemed hard to believe that I had actually been to school with the rest of them.

This reminds me of another photo I have, obviously taken during a school social event. It's a picture of a group of ten- or eleven-year-olds in the bush, eating a picnic. The children are clumped into four small groups, facing inwards and sharing food or talking. All except one child, who sits on the edge of a group, side-on to the other children. She clutches her lunchbox close to her body and looks downwards. This girl is the only one wearing a checked school uniform; all the rest are in jeans and T-shirts or pretty dresses. Did I not know that it was a mufti day, I wonder? I don't remember this outing or how I felt about it, but it's all too easy to guess from my body language.

To me, this photo sums up my relationship to school and indeed to being part of any large social group. I don't know why I was always left out, why I never fitted in. I was quite clever but by no means a high achiever at school. I was terrible at sport and completely unaware of popular culture. I was shy and nervous. I liked reading. Are these reason enough to be an outsider? Or was there something else about me that marked me out?

Twenty cute four-year-olds dressed in reindeer hats sit cross-legged on the floor before Mrs D, who smiles at them and signals to them to rise. Rows of proud parents, some with video cameras in hand, watch as the children start to perform their end-of-year kindergarten concert. I feel more anxious than proud. Ben stands in the front row, his hat falling over his left ear, his face very serious and his mouth closed. The other children sing along to the music but Ben is too busy concentrating on remembering the actions to sing. He moves his arms in a stiff way, just a couple of beats behind the other children. When they twirl around, he ends up facing the wrong way and it takes him several seconds to realise this and shuffle back around to the front. After the singing, the teacher signals for the children to sit down again and they do, except for Ben. The teacher presses gently on his shoulder and he says, 'Oh,' then sits down hurriedly on another child's foot and takes off his reindeer hat. After this, each child is given a certificate and a book. The certificates note some achievement or attribute that the child has brought to their work this year. The principal reads out the certificates, presents the books and shakes each child's hand. The child's parents take their photo and then the child sits back down again next to his or her peers. When it is Ben's turn, he hesitates and has to be encouraged to get up. He looks out at the audience of parents in a slight panic and rushes over to where Robert and I are sitting. His certificate is awarded for his 'interesting imagination and sense of humour'.

'That's one way of describing it,' I say to Robert, as everyone moves to the informal morning tea. Robert looks at me sadly and says, 'He's so different from the other kids, isn't he?'

'Yes, he is,' I say, 'but he did so well.' Unlike Robert, I feel quite happy with today's experience. I'm thrilled that Ben was able to participate in his first little school event and seemed so relaxed and at home. The fact that Ben is willing to stay and eat some of the morning tea, in spite of the crowd of unknown parents and siblings, is a bonus. I consider the difference between my reaction and Robert's and think: I've moved on from comparing Ben with other children and seeing what he can't do, now I'm just happy to see him manage what he can. Later, of course, months and years later, it becomes evident that I will never really escape noticing differences and mourning what is a struggle for my child, though those moments of mourning happen less often and are intermingled with many more moments of joy and pride.

*

Every time I've been to a gathering of parents of disabled children, the issue of schooling has come up. Choosing a school for your child seems to be one of the most fraught decisions parents can make and negotiating with the school once your child is there can cause ongoing challenges. Indeed, schooling is a loaded issue for all parents.

We generally think of school as a site of learning and socialisation for children. But for parents, a child's school is much more than this. It is a site of anxiety because it's an area over which parents have almost no control and often little information. It is a site of judgement because our children – and therefore we ourselves – are measured, compared and evaluated. It is a site of highly charged memories, often negative ones, from our own schooling. For a parent of a disabled child, it is also the first real site of encounter between your child and the wider community. And it is the key site of change – the place where the regular transitions of childhood and then adolescence are marked with events and celebrations.

If your child has a developmental disability, contemplating his schooling is bound to be especially difficult because a school is structured around chronological age. When your child's physical, emotional, social and cognitive development is out of sync with his chronological age, you constantly see him struggling to keep up with his peers. For autistic children there are the additional challenges of sensory overload and what is described as 'the hidden curriculum'. This term is used to describe things that are understood by most children but which confuse a more literal-minded autistic child. For example, the rule 'Walk in the undercover area' means don't run in the undercover area, but is phrased in a way that is confusing to Ben, who often used to ask me, 'Am I allowed to walk in the outside areas, too?' Similarly, 'Look to your classroom teacher for instructions' muddled him because he expected to see instructions and they never appeared. When faced with the maths question 'What is the difference between nine and six?', Ben didn't recognise it as a subtraction question. Instead he answered, 'One is odd and the other is even.' And when his Italian teacher told the class they would be 'taking a trip around Italy', Ben was the only child who rushed home in a panic about travelling without his mum.

Relinquishing control over your child's environment is possibly one of the hardest things for any parent to do. I found it especially hard because I had spent so much time translating between Ben and other people – explaining to him what other people were saying and translating his subtle (and sometimes not so subtle) messages back to others. It was only after I realised that his assistant, Mrs R, understood him that I felt comfortable leaving him. We were incredibly lucky to have Mrs R work with him for the early years of his schooling – it helped him a lot and me even more. Then, of course, I realised we were both dependent on Mrs R and this probably wasn't a good thing. But Ben had developed confidence in himself, his peers and the idea of school. His communication skills improved. By year three he was able to tell me on the first day of school that he was 'only slightly anxious', compared with 'quite anxious' the year before and 'very anxious' at the start of year one. 'Next year I won't be anxious at all,' he informed me. I often think that Ben has a better handle on managing anxiety than I have.

It is assembly time at school and Ben is going to win a merit certificate. He doesn't say much, but I know he is pleased. It's true that he won one last term, but that was for 'trying to improve his handwriting', something Ben doesn't see as important or valuable. The children all sit on mats on the concrete floor and

I sit on one of the benches, not far from Ben. One of the classes does a little skit. Then the student of the month certificates are given out. The children are rewarded for 'courtesy and consideration in the classroom', 'making great strides in class work' and 'representing the school in the community'. Each time another student wins an award, Ben bobs up and down on the mat. Occasionally he turns and looks at me, anxious that he won't get an award after all. I smile and nod at him. Then the principal of the local high school presents the character award, which is only given out every couple of months. Ben's classmate Jamie wins the award for 'helping a friend in need'. Everyone claps and Jamie goes to the front to get his certificate. The principal asks him to tell everyone about 'the friend in need'. Jamie says, 'His name is Ben and I'm teaching him how to play football.' Ben bobs up and turns to look at me again. I smile and nod. Finally, after several more announcements, the weekly merit certificates are given out. Ben wins his for 'showing improvement in his handwriting'. Then the assembly is over: I wave at him as he goes back to class.

As I walk home, I think about what I've just witnessed. Ben has been labelled a child 'in need' in front of the whole school community – students, teachers and parents. He has been told that children who play with him need to be rewarded. And he himself has been rewarded, not for his positive, playful and generous character, not for his remarkable memory, his excellent spelling and maths, nor for the courage and persistence he shows every day. No, he has been rewarded for improved handwriting yet again. At a single stroke, the friendship between Ben and Jamie – which is based on mutual pleasure in each other's company – has been redefined as an unequal relationship of need and charity. Even if this was done quite unconsciously, which I expect it was, nothing changes the message this sends to Ben and his classmates – that Ben's friendship is not valuable, that he is not his peers' equal.

I notice that I also feel a sense of humiliation, as if I have been shown up as a failure because my son is less competent and independent than others his age. Just as disabled children are considered lesser than non-disabled children, so, too, are their mothers. Gail Landsman has argued that the 'diminished personhood of the child with disabilities' is linked to an experience of 'diminished motherhood' for the mother. Because a mother's moral value rests on her association with a valued or 'perfect' child, the mother of a disabled child is not seen as 'morally equivalent'. I felt marked out at the school assembly, as if I had been given a certificate of failure.

It feels like a public branding, even though I tell myself that I am overreacting, that I am too sensitive. But it's the final straw for me. After four years of positive and nurturing experiences at this school, something has changed. I'm not sure if it's the unsympathetic teacher he's had this year, the fact that the charismatic principal has left, the increasing demands of academic work for nine-year-olds, changes in his class group, or a combination of all these factors. But things are not going well. There is the obsession with trying to make him write neatly, when he simply hasn't developed the fine motor skills to be able to do so. There is the failure to develop and implement an Individual Education Plan, even though this is a legal requirement. There is the day his medical file is left open in the classroom so that any student could read it. There is the teacher's refusal to consult with me or Ben's therapists. There is the way he doesn't know how to give Ben useful feedback and simply marks his work as incorrect. There is the inability to understand Ben's sensory needs, so that one day he comes home crying because he's been given one hundred lines to write out at lunchtime as punishment for 'rocking on his chair' in class. And the way he is bullied and the bully suspended and I only hear about it by chance several days later from another student.

Before the end of the year, I find myself at the district office, not filing a formal complaint but raising my concerns. This is not where you want to end up, but sometimes you do. For me, it happens when I sense that Ben's access to an adequate education is being treated as a privilege, not a right. This eventually leads us to our new school and Room 5.

'How was your day?'

'It was good,' says Ben. This is what he answers just about every day, so I don't know why I keep asking him the question.

'Did you go to the library?'

'Yes, of course. I found a book on magic.'

'Oh! Anything else interesting happen?' I probe.

'Not really, it was just a normal Friday.'

Of course, I don't actually know what a 'normal Friday' is like at school, but I take Ben's point – he has nothing particular to tell me. Nonetheless, just as we turn into our driveway, Ben says, 'Mum, remember yesterday we counted the seeds in the pumpkin and measured its circumference in maths? Well, today we made pumpkin scones.'

'Really? That sounds like fun. Did you eat them?'

'Yes, we did. They were good.'

'You do fun things at school,' I say to Ben.

'Yes, we do.'

'And what did you do at lunchtime?' I ask.

'I ate my lunch and then I practised running on the oval.'

'Oh. Did you run races?'

'No, I just practised on my own.' By this time, we're out of the car and walking to the back door. I turn and look at Ben.

'Were you happy on your own then, Ben?'

'Yes, I was happy,' he says. 'And besides, I had to practise my running.' And he looks relaxed about it. He doesn't seem sad that he plays on his own a lot at lunchtime. Is this because he doesn't feel sad or lonely or because he doesn't recognise those feelings or because he's covering up his feelings? I don't ask because I don't want to make a big deal out of it or make him feel uncomfortable. I don't want to impose my own experiences and feelings onto his. I start singing a song about pumpkin scones and Ben smiles. 'Join in,' I suggest and he sings along. His singing voice is sweet and in tune, a sound that only I ever hear.

Thinking about my own loneliness as a child, the distinction researchers make between emotional loneliness and social-cognitive loneliness makes sense. According to Robert Weiss, emotional loneliness is the result of a failure to bond with others and leads to feelings of sadness, fear and emptiness. This is the loneliness of a child without close family connections and affection. Social-cognitive loneliness arises when we are excluded from social networks or peer groups. This results in feelings of exclusion and marginality. Because I had very close bonds with my siblings as a child, I wasn't emotionally lonely generally, but rather felt acutely excluded at school. I was self-conscious and ashamed as well as sad about this exclusion, and so never spoke about these feelings at home.

Although I have suffered from loneliness as both a child and an adult, I find myself seeking out solitariness quite often. I have travelled alone, lived alone and run my own business. I find myself drawn to solitary activities such as writing and reading. One of my secret pleasures is to go to the movies on my own, though why it should be secret I don't know. I suppose that I still feel the sense that others may judge me for being solitary. Perhaps I judge myself. In spite of my desire for time alone, I do treasure my close friends and family, and value and enjoy intimacy with others enormously.

Perhaps Ben is similar. He loves to be with family and friends and he seems to enjoy school. But he also likes lots of time alone in his bedroom, reading, writing, using his computer or listening to music. The difference seems to be that Ben doesn't experience that sense of exclusion that I felt as a child. Or perhaps he recognises his marginal status but doesn't find it upsetting. I have seen research that suggests that autistic children experience more loneliness than their non-autistic peers but express less sadness about this than other children. This lack of sadness is put down to their 'lack of understanding' of loneliness or of the 'social deficits' of autism. Is it really a deficit, though, that enables someone to feel comfortable even though they are not included in a social grouping? Is it a deficit to be able to find meaning in your own life, regardless of your status in larger social networks?

In spite of my admiration for Ben's independence and resilience, I still want him to play with other kids at school. I hate the thought of him always being on his own and on the margins. As Heinrich Pestalozzi said, 'You can drive the devil out of your garden but you will find him again in the garden of your son.' I don't think I'll ever finish struggling with my feelings of loneliness and exclusion. But I do realise now that these are my demons, not Ben's. He will no doubt have his own life-long struggles. But for now, I think he is content and safe, running alone on the oval at lunchtime, reading about magic and making pumpkin scones.

FROG IN GIRLLAND

There is no greater agony than bearing an untold story inside you.
—MAYA ANGELOU

'MUM, MY MAIN HOBBY is writing adventure stories, so I'll be doing that while you drive.'

'Good idea. It's lucky you like writing because it's a long way,' I say, still apprehensive about the prospect of five hours with a ten-year-old boy in the back of the car.

'That's okay, Mum. I'm only on number ten of twenty-five volumes of my Frog and Girlland stories.'

'Oh, I see. You're going to do twenty-five books, are you?' In my mind's eye, I see the stack of exercise books – already knee high in Ben's bedroom – rising to the ceiling, each one filled with handwritten and illustrated stories.

'Yes. I did eight Frog and Toad books, and ten Rowena Smithtwinson books, and I'm going to do twenty-five Frog and Girlland books. There are more Frog and Girlland books because they're an ensemble series. Ensemble means there are lots of characters, not just one.'

'Yes.' I don't know why Ben sometimes talks to me as though I know nothing.

'And then I might do a new series,' he continues.

'Oh? What will the new series be?'

'It's about a dog called Growler.'

'Growler!' I exclaim, in mock horror. Ben knows I don't like dogs.

'Don't worry, he's only a made-up dog. And besides, he's gentle. The first one is called "Growler the Dog" and the next one is "Growler and the Triplets". How many Growler books do you think I should do?'

'I don't know, Ben. But you don't have to decide now. Just wait and see how you feel.'

There's a pause while I drive and Ben writes. Then he says, 'Mum, I'm going to put a note to the reader at the end of the last Frog and Girlland book. They might be sad not to read about the characters any more so I'm going to say that these characters will be in the Growler series as well.'

'Good idea, that will be reassuring,' I say, though I wonder if I'm guilty of encouraging Ben to live in a fantasy world. After all, these 'readers' he speaks of are only his family, really. He talks about his stories as if they are or will be published children's books rather than a stack of handwritten pages in his bedroom. Then again, don't all of us fantasise about our own creations being widely read and enjoyed?

I'm more struck these days by Ben's similarity to me than his difference. Here we are, driving down south for a week's holiday, and both of us have packed books to read and blank notebooks to write in. Our clothes and other packing took much less time than choosing appropriate books and checking that our five pens all work properly!

'What about a pack of cards or Monopoly?' I suggested, so Ben darted into his bedroom and added them to the pile.

'Now I'm ready,' he announced, clutching his book and pen.

'What about totem tennis or a football or your scooter or something like that? We have space.'

'I'll take the scooter,' he agreed, not really interested, but being helpful.

'Now we need your portable DVD player and some DVDs and CDs,' I said. 'I don't want you getting bored in the car and asking me if we're there yet every five minutes.'

'Okay,' he sighed and went off to get them, like a parent humouring a troublesome child.

Now we're on the road and all I have to do is fill up with petrol before we leave the city. I pull into a Caltex station and Ben comes in with me when I pay, still holding his pen and tucking his notebook under his jacket just in case the threatened rain eventuates. When we're back in the car, he says, 'Mum, I have a new character: Skip Caltex. He's American and his face is shaped like the star on the Caltex logo.'

I laugh, but he doesn't seem to mind. He's scribbling away again, muttering under his breath, immersed in Frog and Girlland.

By the time we reach Williams, I'm ready for a break and Ben has finished his Skip Caltex story. He brings his book into the café with him and reads me the beginning.

Skip Caltex really enjoyed his life. For breakfast he got to make these really tasty lemon and sugar pancakes, he always got his favourite dessert, two chocolate chip cookies and a glass of milk from another country to dip them in.

'It says cookies because Skip is American,' Ben explains.

But one day, Skip's parents had bad news. The Caltex family had to move house because Skip's dad had to get a new job. The trouble was, near the new house there were lots of girls in the neighbourhood. Skip Caltex didn't like girls because they teased him.

'Oh dear,' I say. 'I wonder why they teased him?'

'He was a show-off,' explains Ben.

My coffee and Ben's muffin arrive at this point, so we put

the book safely away from possible spills.

'You can tell me the rest of the story,' I say, sipping my coffee.

'Skip has to go to a new school and he's worried.'

'Oh, just like you – starting a new school this year.' I like it when Ben's stories draw on his own life.

'But it's all okay in the end, Mum, because he saves the school swimming instructor from drowning. He likes school after that. And he gets a new girlfriend.' Ben takes a large bite of muffin.

'A new girlfriend. Who's that?'

'Rhiannon Submerge, of course. Skip makes her lemon and sugar pancakes.'

'Yum! We should try making pancakes down south,' I suggest.

'I'm going to write a story about Nina O'Frogger going to prison next,' announces Ben.

'Prison! My goodness!' I don't think this story will be drawn from life. I drink my coffee, Ben eats his muffin.

For almost a year, Ben called me 'Toad'. I know exactly why he did this and I know it wasn't because of my looks, but none-theless I initially found it uncomfortable. Images of moist scabby skin, bulging eyes and prehensile feet slid through my mind.

Ben was 'Frog' and this I had no trouble with, because frogs seem endearing and likeable creatures. We have a fish pond in the garden and sometimes we spot beautiful little frogs resting on the lily pads. We hear them at night as they call for a mate. Occasionally, after a hot night, Ben discovers a frog swimming around in his paddling pool in the morning and we scoop it up into a plastic bowl and then lower it gently into the pond, whereupon it immediately flashes its long legs and disappears under debris at the bottom.

Frog and Toad came into being when Ben was five years old and I read him a series of stories by Arnold Lobel about a frog and a toad who are best friends. We both loved these stories – we still do – because they have a wonderful inventive innocence about them. Toad is always getting into minor difficulties – he loses a button, he worries about where Frog is, he is upset he never gets letters, he can't stop eating cookies, he doesn't want others to see him in his bathers. Frog is slightly wiser and more worldly – he knows when spring is around the corner, he understands willpower, he knows how to test bravery. Ben immediately connected to Frog and Toad, casting himself as the clever Frog and me as the confused Toad, a casting that I initially felt was faulty but which over the years I have recognised to be correct.

We started off by acting out Lobel's stories, mimicking the dialogue word for word. Fairly soon, though, Ben branched out and started retelling our own life events as Frog and Toad stories. By calling me Toad and himself Frog, he enabled himself to talk about his thoughts, feelings and actions in the third person.

'Let's tell about our day,' he would say, and I would start a story.

'Well, today when Toad picked Frog up from pre-primary, Mrs W said that Frog had had an accident.'

'What had Frog done?'

'Frog had seen a bucket of water and put his head into it. Poor Frog didn't know the water was full of detergent for making bubbles.'

'How did Frog feel?'

'Well, I don't know. How did Frog feel?'

'It hurt poor Frog's eyes. Mrs W washed his eyes and gave him a tea towel. Then he was okay.'

'I expect Frog will think more carefully before he puts his head into a bucket again.' I was never averse to using these retells as a way of imprinting sensible behaviour.

'I don't think Frog was *naughty*, was he?' Ben, too, had his way of using stories to make sense of the day.

I could see that Ben found it much easier to talk about Frog's experiences than to directly own them. He wouldn't agree, for example, that his eyes had hurt after being in the bucket, but he could agree that Frog's eyes had hurt, while at the same time, it was clear to both of us that Frog was Ben in this story. It was as if the distancing that third person created helped Ben integrate an experience or event and the feelings that went with it.

After only a few weeks, Ben completely identified as Frog and only ever called me Toad, never Mummy as he previously had. When strangers asked him his name he replied in all seriousness, 'Frog'. I got some very strange looks from people, wondering what sort of a mother would give her child such a name. At the start of pre-primary one day, Ben called to me, using the name Toad, to ask for help. A little boy turned to me, saying, 'I thought you were called Rachel. Why did he call you Toad?' Another time, an acquaintance said to me, in front of Ben, 'Your little boy must be about six now, I'd guess?' Ben replied quite crossly, 'I'm not a boy, I'm a green tree frog. And I am not six, I'm five.' This was how I discovered that Ben wasn't just any old frog, but a particular species. It was also, I think, the first time I connected Ben's fear of turning six with his insistence on being Frog.

As his sixth birthday approached, Ben became more and more adamant that he wouldn't be turning six. I kept reassuring him that nothing changes just because your age advances, but he wouldn't have it. Frog wanted to stay five forever.

'But what about a birthday party?' I asked. 'How can you have a party if you don't change age?'

'I'll have an un-birthday party.'

'What about presents? Don't you want any?'

'I'll have presents, just not birthday presents.'

So, we did have a party on Ben's birthday and asked his friends not to say 'happy birthday' to him. They gave him presents but we all maintained the pretence that they had nothing to do with turning six. He still described himself as five if anyone asked.

This desire to create a different reality with words is not limited to Ben or to children in general. As adults, many of us fall into this type of magical thinking – if I don't name something, it doesn't exist. I think it must be a protective mechanism; sometimes we need to delay facing reality for a little bit longer. Perhaps Ben needed to put off facing the fact of being a six-year-old boy, about to start year one. He wanted to stay as five-year-old Frog, having wonderful times with his best friend Toad.

Researchers used to claim that autistic people have impoverished imaginations and an inability to be creative. In fact, some researchers still argue this and one of the diagnostic criteria for an autism spectrum disorder remains 'delayed or abnormal functioning' in the area of 'symbolic or imaginative play'. But more recently, there has come to be an acceptance that some autistic people, especially those with language, have rich imaginative inner worlds and can produce creative ideas and works. As if to prove this, many artists, thinkers and scientists (for example, Einstein, Wittgenstein, Bartók and Beethoven) have been retrospectively 'claimed' as autistic. There are also autistic savants, who demonstrate extreme skills in one area such as music, mathematics or drawing, sometimes involving imaginative or creative skills, sometimes not.

Still, much of the behaviour and conversation of autistic children does seem to be rigid, repetitive and pedestrian – the very opposite of the imaginative flights of fancy exhibited by neurotypical children. I found myself reading a research paper recently in which it was reported that children with autism, in contrast to typically developing children, 'failed at drawing impossible pictures'! I can quite see how Ben would fail at drawing the impossible (by which the researchers meant fantastical or non-real). His illustrations of Frog and Toad are wonderfully idiosyncratic and capture something particular to our experience (Toad's face when cross bears an uncanny resemblance to mine), but they remain tethered to the notion of amphibians. There are no space-age characters or people with wings or other 'impossible' drawings. And the variation within his stories is not great. Frog gets lost and found; Frog is naughty and Toad gets angry; the characters of Frog and Girlland go to school, have adventures and then come home for tea.

Oliver Sacks compares Coleridge's descriptions of Fancy and Imagination. While Fancy manipulates fixed, ready-made materials, Imagination 'dissolves, diffuses, dissipates, in order to recreate'. Sacks suggests that the letting go of fixities and creating something new that is true imagination is difficult for the 'overprecise and rigid mind of an autistic person'. I see this in Ben – a powerful attachment to the concrete and given, and the desire to replay familiar elements many times until he has exhausted them and moves on. Frog got lost in about twenty stories before, finally, a new motif emerged. Was Ben feeling lost at that time? Possibly, and possibly this was the only way he could tell us that. Similarly, we enacted many times the moment in *The Wind and the Willows* when Rat dances up and down on the road shouting 'You villains ... You scoundrels, you highway-men, you – you – road-hogs! I'll have the law on you!' at a car driver, while Toad sits by the roadside entranced by a vision of the motor car. Was this scene fascinating to Ben because it is funny (he found it hilarious), or because it gave him the chance to jump up and down in mock-fury, or because he himself has experienced a sudden interest in something new, like Toad? These things I don't know. I only know that quotes from Kenneth Grahame were a part of our life for several years, and that many a time we have startled strangers with comments about 'biscuits, potted lobster, sardines – everything you can possibly want' or 'like summer tempests came his tears'.

One of the earliest signs of autism in a young child is a lack of interest in 'pretend play'. The classic example of this is an autistic boy lining up toy cars or spinning their wheels but never pushing them along an imaginary road or putting a toy character inside the car. This lack of pretend play is seen as evidence of limited imagination, though it is clear that when they grow older many children who failed to take part in imaginative play do develop some imaginative and creative capacities. These may include a love of painting, making up unusual words or phrases, building things, making creative messes, even finding creative ways to break the rules or escape constraints. If you are an autistic person in a neurotypical world, simply getting through each day can be an act of creativity. As disabled dancer Neil Marcus has said, 'Disability is an art. It's an ingenious way to live.' Tito Mukhopadhyay, an autistic poet, has described how he used the power of his imagination to cope with the world, for example, by imagining himself to be travelling inside a mirror: 'Mirror travel was a part of my day's work ... It was a sort of an escape from situations and I could form my own little stories behind it by looking through it.'

If being creative is seeing the same thing as everybody else but thinking of something different, then I'd say lots of autistic people are creative. The ability to focus attention in that single-minded way that some autistics have can result in new discoveries, different connections and a new aesthetics. These, however, may not always be viewed as valuable in the neurotypical world. How many paintings of electric light switches will an art gallery hang?

Bruce Mills has argued that Western concepts of the imagination from the Romantic era onwards have emphasised its ability to unify and generalise. He too points to Coleridge, who described imagination as a way of turning individual events or memories into new scenarios and stories. Discrete experiences are valued more when they are transformed into broader sweeps of narrative. Mills suggests that we value imagination for two particular things: its capacity to organise information into unified categories and its ability to express inner psychological states. He points out that these two aspects link to two theories about autism. The central coherence theory suggests that autistic people can't generalise or unify. The theory of mind hypothesis argues that autistic people can't understand the feelings and beliefs of other people. In other words, Mills is suggesting that our understanding of imagination is a neurotypical one.

What would happen if we applied a different set of values to our understanding of imagination and creativity? What if we valued individual, concrete manifestations rather than unifying ones? Mills suggests that if we made this conceptual shift we would discover 'an imaginative faculty defined by close attention to mechanical or physical patterns not psychological or social rules, by a private not public symbol structure, and by an internal integrity or unity evolving in part from idiosyncratic sensory preferences'. He argues that such a shift is necessary if we are to recognise the special skills and contributions of autistic people.

I think I know what Mills means here. For some months, Ben became very interested in drains and began drawing pictures of the different drain configurations (actually, there aren't that many). He seemed to experience an aesthetic pull to look at and reproduce drains. It was something to do with the shape of them, the inner lines and the outer circle and how they connected. It didn't mean anything: there was no bigger story or point to this interest from my perspective, but it was meaningful to Ben. I didn't consider Ben's drain drawings as art; they didn't get stuck up on the fridge the way his occasional flower drawings from school did. But wasn't that my lack of vision, my inflexibility? When I think about it, drains and flowers are not that dissimilar in shape, but my response to pictures of them is very different, perhaps reflecting that Romantic view of the imagination.

All the same, I'm glad he moved on from drains fairly quickly. Frog and Girlland I find much more appealing. Oliver Sacks (agreeing with Coleridge) says, 'Creativity has to do with inner life – with the flow of new ideas and strong feelings.' To me, Ben's illustrated stories about Frog are exactly that – they reveal his latest ideas and feelings about things that are meaningful to him.

'Stop the rain!'

'I can't stop the rain. Only the clouds can do that.'

'Tell the clouds to stop raining, then,' reads Ben.

'It doesn't work like that. We can't stop the rain.'

'What a terrible world it is when we can't even stop the rain,' Ben moans.

'Poor Frog, you feel very sad,' I read.

'Yes, I do feel sad,' says Ben, hamming up the sad voice.

'You feel alone in your sadness.'

'Yes, I do feel alone.'

'You feel angry that I can't stop the rain,' I read.

'Yes, I do feel angry,' says Ben, now making his 'cross' face.

'You feel scared that no one can control the rain.'

'Yes, I do feel scared.'

'You wonder how you can feel safe in such a big world, full of rain and other things you don't like.'

'Yes, I do wonder.'

'You feel like sitting here and crying all day,' I read.

'No!' exclaims Ben, enjoying his punchline. 'I don't feel like crying all day. I think I have had enough of crying now.'

'Oh! What shall we do then?'

'I think we will go outside and splash in the puddles,' says Ben, smiling broadly.

'And so the two friends went outside into the rain and splashed in the puddles and got very muddy together,' I read.

'The End,' finishes Ben.

We are reading – yet again – a story I wrote for Ben called 'Frog and Toad Talk about the Rain'. It is written somewhat in the style of Arnold Lobel and I have printed it in colour, including some pictures of Frog and Toad. In the story, Frog is crying about the rain and Toad is trying to comfort him. Toad tries logical reasoning, but it doesn't work. He tries to distract Frog with a story, some food and a song, but this doesn't work either. Eventually Toad asks Frog in despair what he can do to make Frog feel better and this is when Frog asks Toad to stop the rain.

I wrote this story for Ben the same winter he was determined to stay five. Even now, all these years later, we sometimes revisit it and read it together, just for fun. It wasn't written for fun, though, but to try to deal with Ben's anxiety and distress. That winter, Ben became very disturbed when it rained or when he thought it might rain. He would throw himself onto the ground, wherever we were, and scream or run into his bedroom, get into bed and cry. I never really understood what caused this distress but I think perhaps it related to one of his passions of the time, which was using chalk to write numbers around the garden. Ben would spend many hours a day (if I let him) recreating rows of letterbox numbers. It was like repeating all those walks around the neighbourhood that we'd done the year before. Only now, he would recreate them in his head and transpose them onto the walls of the house, the paving stones, the fences, and the odd bricks and stakes of wood around our large and shambolic garden. After he'd drawn the letterboxes and written in the numbers, he'd take me by the hand and walk me around the garden to see each street, so that I'd be ducking under tree branches to admire unusually shaped letterboxes and peering at chalk numbers squashed between corrugations in the fence, pretending to remember the actual house that we once saw six months ago on a specific street. When he'd exhausted one particular walk, he would ask me to wash the numbers off so that he could start again with a new street. I knew that some people rather wondered about all these numbers on the walls of the house, but I thought it was quite colourful and in any case, a lot better than fighting over writing on walls inside the house!

I think Ben worried about the rain washing off his numbers, even though he was going to do so himself after a while. We talked about it, but he couldn't tell me why rain or the thought of rain sent him into a state of near panic. This was when I wrote the Frog and Toad story.

I wasn't sure whether this story would make a difference to Ben, but the first night I read it to him, he loved it. He laughed and got me to read it several more times. The next night he decided to read Frog's dialogue, hamming up the emotions with great relish, while I read the narration and Toad's dialogue. Over the next week or so, Ben's dread of the rain dissipated. He didn't enjoy the rain, but he stopped obsessively thinking about and fearing it. We never talked about how the story might have changed his feelings. I didn't want to address it directly in case the effect wore off. I don't know why reading the story helped where discussion hadn't. It was as though it meant nothing to him that his mum empathised but as soon as Toad did, he felt better. I wrote a couple of other stories – one about Frog's fear of dogs and one about the fear of change called 'Frog Wants Forever'. Ben liked both stories and understood the messages, but I don't think they were as effective as the rain story.

And then I felt that Ben was growing out of Frog and Toad. He gradually resumed his own name and started calling me Mum. (I was relieved not to be Toad but I missed Mummy, the name only young children use and which I experienced for such a short while.) I thought maybe we had seen the last of Frog and Toad, but I was wrong. Ben stopped being Frog, but he still identified with Frog. As he explained to me one day, 'Mum, I used to say I was Frog, but really it was my nickname.' He understood that his previous adoption of Frog was different from his current feeling about Frog. It was as though he no longer needed Frog as a way to exist. He could now reflect back on his old self and his current self and see the difference. He could say 'I' about himself now, so that if he was telling me something that happened in school, he would now say, 'I saw this' or (a year or so later) 'I felt that.'

*

Ben helped me see the strong connection between narrative and identity. If we cannot tell stories about ourselves and our world, it seems we cannot really develop a sense of self, a sense that we are a unique individual in a world of many selves. In his book *How Our Lives Become Stories*, Paul John Eakin argues that 'narrative plays a central structuring role in the formation and maintenance of our sense of identity'. We narrate our life and, in doing so, we narrate ourselves into existence. In everyday life, we understand ourselves through a kind of ongoing story. We reference our past all the time when we talk about ourselves. Without a sense of our own past and a possible future, we seem to have no continuity of self.

In his work with people with neurological damage, Oliver Sacks notes how much we need this inner life story, how we are, in a sense, our own narrative. This is why people with profound amnesia or advanced Alzheimer's disease are described as being 'not themselves' or without a self.

Autistic people have also been described as 'unselved' or 'differently selved'. Sidonie Smith, for example, argues that autism challenges this notion of narrating identity. Some autistic people are unable to create a memory-based story of their lives. Smith asks if a diagnosis of autism in effect consigns these individuals to an unautobiographical life. Do they become in some way an 'unnarratable self'?

These are interesting questions, but I wonder if they are based on a notion that stories can only be language-based? What about a story of the self that is told in pictures or bodily movements? Would that be sufficient to construct an identity? Ben and other autistic children I've met use objects and move their bodies in different ways from other children. Ben does a lot of tapping and circling, which is interesting to watch once in a while but can also drive me crazy. Lots of people tap and circle, but Ben's movements are very characteristic. To me, they form at least part of a very personal story.

Developmental psychologists have shown that children start to tell their own stories with the development of language and what is described as 'memory talk'. This is when the child first discovers the use of memory to understand the past, see patterns and therefore predict the future. From this time onwards the child will remember more autobiographical events, as they now have a function – they help to predict the future. As more language is acquired, an understanding of time and how to talk about time also develops.

Eakin argues that the development of autobiographical memory in early childhood prepares for the writing of autobiography in adult life. He cites research by Dennie Palmer Wolf, who traces the emergence of 'an authorial self' between the ages of two and four, and shows how children learn to manipulate memories by retelling the same event in different ways. The child masters the double point of view of retrospect, learning to speak as both subject and object.

What happens, then, to a child who has not developed language in the typical way or at the expected stage? What about a child like Ben, who didn't seem able to distinguish between himself and others at the age of two or three? One of the things I noticed when Ben was young was his lack of instinctive understanding of the boundaries of consciousness between self and other. It was as if he had no notion of a private self (and thus no notion that others might have private selves). How do you tell your child a story about himself if he doesn't appear to possess a level of self-awareness that separates 'you' from 'I'?

I puzzled over these issues when Ben was young. I read all the literature that suggested that autistic people can't form narratives, that autistic people have a different type of consciousness, that autistic people don't have a sense of self, that autistic children may not develop language in a way that allows for the authorial self, that autistic people cannot write their own autobiography. I also read autobiographies and websites written by autistic people. And I listened to Ben, his growing understanding of himself and the world and how he told and then wrote stories to help himself understand and grow from his experiences.

I watched how Ben's first stories were simple Frog and Toad stories: Frog gets lost, they visit the swimming pool, Toad gets cross. How they developed into more complex stories, including Mero the Magic Cat and Mr Spud. How, among all the repetitions and all the many numbers, clocks, playing cards and calendars, were wonderfully poetic phrases and evocative images.

On Sunday I followed a maze and got lost. I lost my pen! Then I went to a park and I swung so high on a swing. The wind blew into my mouth! All day I carried an easterly wind in my mouth.

I noticed how Frog and Toad turned into Frog and Girlland as Ben aged and Toad (his mum) was less important than girls with wonderful names like Arianna Squidgrain, Angelina Divisions and Paraphenalia Carnation. How not long afterwards boys started to join Frog and the girls in Girlland. How his illustrations got smaller and less frequent and the stories longer and more interesting.

I observed how Ben gradually involved readers in his stories with notes to 'fans', fun quizzes, word searches and codes to break at the back of his stories. How he started decorating the front covers of his books and writing blurbs on the back: *At the school open day everyone is going to be on their best behaviour. Or are they? Read this story and find out.* I saw that some of Ben's stories became meta-fictional, as the author/narrator broke out of the text and started to become a character (*As for me, the author, I just sat in my chair, smiling, and said 'Frog and Girlland Rocks!'*) and the characters began to speak to the author and disagree with the way the plot was going (*'I'd better talk to the author,' said John, 'I need a more interesting name'*).

I watched all this and I stopped reading about autism, narrative and identity.

'Mum, I'm going to take a break from writing now.'

'Good idea, Ben. You can watch a DVD or listen to music if you like.' I'm thrilled with how the drive has gone. We've only stopped twice and all the rest of the time Ben has been happily writing his stories or reading or just sitting in the back chatting to me. We even had a laugh over my story about when he was younger and he threw a box of hot chips over the front seat at me. Ben promises me he would never do that now. I know that his psychologist believes that Ben's keen interest in writing stories is an obsession or 'perseveration', as she calls it. There is a lot of repetition in the stories and he does it with great focus. She doesn't tell me to stop him writing but she does encourage me to challenge and interrupt the writing and steer him towards spontaneous interactions with others. Much as I respect her expertise, I don't quite agree with her on this matter, because writing stories doesn't seem like an inappropriate obsession to me. I see it as a genuine form of self-expression and a way to work through complex issues. It may also be a substitute for more social interaction, and this makes me sad. I wish I could magic up a series of lovely children who want nothing more than to spend time with Ben, but I can't. Given that, I'm very happy that Ben has found a rewarding channel for his desires. I think most people who love to read and write actually learned to do so because they were lonely. I know I did.

'By the way,' I say, 'how did Nina O'Frogger go in prison?'

'She didn't like it, so she escaped.'

'How did she do that?'

'Skip Caltex and Rhiannon Submerge helped her,' he explains, 'because they're her friends. Friends should help each other, don't you think, Mum?'

'Yes, I do, Ben.'

We drive on.

FANCY FOOTWORK

The meeting of two personalities is like the contact of two chemical substances: if there is any reaction, both are transformed.
—CARL JUNG

WHEN BEN STARTED HIS new school recently, he was asked to complete a brief questionnaire to help the teacher get to know him. Whereas most of the questions were specific, like 'What is your favourite subject?', one simply said 'Your family'. Ben wrote: 'My family are people I can rely on and I love them also. I like doing odd jobs for them.' I'm guessing that the teacher expected information about who he lives with, if he has any siblings or grandparents and so on, but I love Ben's answer. It seems complete. What else do we need to know about family except that we love them, we can rely on them and they can rely on us?

It was especially moving to see Ben write this comment because psychologists argue that autistic people are often unable to form close relationships with others, unable to self-reflect and unable to empathise with others or consider their needs. Having known Ben for a decade, I know that he is capable of love, empathy and self-reflection, although the way he experiences and expresses these things is likely to be very different from how I and other neurotypicals do.

Reading his comment about family makes me realise that Ben is the person I feel most connected to in the world. I'm not talking about the fact that I love him most – which I do – but about intimacy. The fact that this has not always been the case, and that our intimacy is often disrupted and fragmented, that distance often co-exists with this intimacy, does not diminish my sense of connection to him. But it does complicate things, so that we do a continual dance of closeness and separation, with me feeling that I have to do most of the fancy footwork while Ben wanders about only half recognising the dance.

I have no idea whether this is a common feeling for other mothers, especially single mothers. I've had to work hard to get to know Ben and perhaps this has made me aware of things that other mothers – mothers of typically developing children – don't notice. When your child pushes you aside like a piece of unwanted furniture in order to spend hours alone gazing rapt at a row of garden pebbles, all your unexamined assumptions about intimacy, about reciprocity, about love, all are shattered and tossed into the air. This is when the real work of mothering begins. Your child is two, you have weathered seven hundred and thirty sleepless nights, changed six thousand nappies, breast-fed through cracked and torn nipples, pored over twenty-five child development books, mashed numerous pumpkins and apples, tried to turn the baby's cries down with the television remote control ... In short, you have done what all mothers do and yet you haven't even started to learn how to mother your child, because your child appears to be changing in front of your very eyes, won't even meet your eyes, seems to be disappearing off into a parallel world, a mysterious place you soon realise you must try to go yourself, although you can never really get there. This is the start of the dance of intimacy with an autistic child.

*

I remember the first time Ben told me he loved me. He was three and a half years old and because of the way he said it, I knew it was a genuine expression of feeling rather than just another of the repetitive phrases that characterised so much of his conversation at that time. He was still occasionally muddling his pronouns then and so when he said, 'You love Mummy', I knew that it was a deliberate expression of love for me. I knew he loved me, but he did not express his love in the way most children do. When he was upset, he would turn away from me, as if I would be useless as a comforter. He would back into my arms for a hug rather than face me. He didn't respond to his name, look up when I came into the house, or join in any activities with me. He often rejected my advances or pushed me away. I knew that this wasn't about lack of love, but sometimes it felt like it, and it triggered painfully raw feelings in me. What did it say about me that my own (and only) child rejected me? What could provide clearer evidence that I had failed as a mother, that I was unloveable? At such times, all the skeletons in the private cupboard of your psyche are laid bare, their bones madly rattling.

How do we learn the art of intimacy? Is it in fact an art, or can scientists explain how it works? I've used the term intimacy because it implies both closeness and communication. It is something different from attachment – that more clinical term used to describe the mother–child bond. Intimacy is a word more often used in connection with close friends or lovers. By intimacy, I suppose I mean something different from the caring love between mother and son. I mean a type of connection that is less dependent on dependency, a reciprocal relationship that is created and nurtured by both people. Intimacy involves sharing the self. Maternal attachment may be necessary for this sharing to occur between mother and child, but other things are necessary too: spontaneity, empathy, a sense of self and other, an understanding of reciprocity, the ability to participate in moments of intensity or seeming unity with the other, valuing a relationship for its own sake, not its utility. Listing these requirements, I may as well be listing what psychologists describe as the deficits of autism spectrum disorders. Sometimes I have felt that Ben seemed immune to all these things, that he has no concept of me as a person and values me only as a function, someone useful to him. But at other times I have had to revise my thoughts and recognise that it may be the way he expresses his feelings that makes me feel this.

I remember now that what I most feared when Ben was first diagnosed – apart, that is, from fear of the unknown, of not being a good enough mother, and a kind of gut fear that everything I had known for four decades was being torn from me – apart from these fears, my greatest fear was that Ben wouldn't be able to form loving relationships with other people. I had absolutely no doubt that I would love him and that he would, in some way at least, love me. But I feared that what I valued most in my life, my relationships with my partner, my child, my family and my friends, would not be available to him. I couldn't conceive of a meaningful life where these types of relationships weren't fundamental.

I see now that my inability to reconceive my notion of a meaningful life is not uncommon. It is really no different from another person's inability to conceive of life after the loss of a limb, and it mainly derives from ignorance and the lack of a public discourse that shows the diversity of people's lives. Now, it is much easier for me to see how a life with few or no intimate relationships can be meaningful.

Jim Sinclair, an autistic rights activist, says:

I can go for days or weeks without any personal contact with other human beings, and I may get bored but I don't get lonely. I don't need social contact ... Even when someone does attract my interest, when I do become emotionally attached and desire a relationship with that person, I don't become dependent on that relationship or that person. I don't need them.

But wait ... Because I don't need relationships with *anyone*, I'm free to choose a relationship with a *someone* – not because I need a relationship, but because I like that person. When I make contact with someone, it's special.

Sinclair has written eloquently about his life and how he enjoys it and finds it meaningful. He finds understanding other people difficult but he is happy to be autistic and believes his own life to be as valid as anyone else's: 'My selfhood is undamaged. I find great value and meaning in my life, and I have no wish to be cured of being myself.' Many other autistic people have written similarly about their lives, whether they are sometimes solitary like Sinclair or more social. Most autistic people who write autobiographies or blogs or post contributions online talk about how important friendships and family members are, in spite of the difficulties that can surround these relationships. Their words have shown me how there are many different ways to create and live a meaningful life.

And when Ben came to me the other day aglow with the discovery of a new category of numbers called co-primes, I could see how meaningful this was to him, what value it had for him. He brought this discovery to me – he wanted to share it. And so,

I feel now that for Ben, part of life's meaning will be his relationships with others.

I can see, too, that for all my increased understanding of other ways of living, of neurodiversity, I still catch myself thinking in absolute terms. You value relationships or you don't. You care about people or about things. Autistic people are one thing; neurotypicals another. This just isn't how it is. Even accepting that neurological differences are now scientifically verifiable, autism is still only a socially and culturally constructed concept; it's simply a list of behaviours that are classified as symptoms of a medical 'disorder'.

The difficult thing about talking or writing about emotions and autism is that all our language is used in ways that neurotypicals have established, so that our definition of empathy, say, is a neurotypical definition, based on neurotypical behaviours and interpretations. We use it to refer to our automatic reaction to the observed experiences of others. It involves the ability to recognise what another person might be feeling, the ability to assume their perspective (what we call 'walking in their shoes') and an emotional response to this, which is usually similar to the emotional response of the person we are watching.

There are some interesting discussions about empathy posted online between people who self-identify or have been diagnosed as autistic. For example, SavedAspie says:

> Perhaps people don't think Autistics have empathy because we are not wired the same way, and so don't express empathy the way they would.
>
> A lot of people are very surprised to find out how much I care about them. Despite the depths to which I am concerned about my friends and associates, I have a lot of trouble communicating this to them.

It's a hot topic, not just because empathy is seen to be important for relating to people, but also because empathy is often considered to be essential for unselfish behaviour. Philosophically, it may be related to morality and conscience. It is understandable that autistic people would feel uncomfortable about being described as without empathy and therefore the will to do good to others. Empathy is also closely related to the notion of theory of mind, another concept hotly debated among autism researchers and autistic people. Theory of mind refers to our ability to understand the feelings, intentions and motivations of others. The idea is that, in fact, neurotypicals don't need a theory because we do it instinctively, but that autistic people are 'mind-blind'. Does empathy require theory of mind? It's unclear.

The distinction between the capacity to recognise emotions in another, to feel emotions in response to this and to show these emotions in predictable (neurotypical) ways seems clear to autistic people but not always to neurotypicals. Joel Smith says:

> I know I'm not always the most sensitive person. But that hardly means that I don't have empathy or that I can't imagine myself in someone else's place. In fact, much of my day, interacting with neurotypicals, I find I must imagine things through someone else's eyes – a form of empathy. To be honest, I think neurotypicals do less of this than autistic people do, as most of the people around them most of the time think like they do. Neurotypicals don't usually need to run with their translation system on full power.
>
> ... We also have different responses when confronted with, for instance, someone who is sad. For me, it is overwhelming, threatening to wash my being away, when

someone I care about is upset. The only thing I can do is to freeze and look into myself. This isn't because I don't realise someone is suffering, it is instead because they are suffering. I feel the pain very deeply. A differing response to that pain doesn't mean that pain isn't felt!

Jim Sinclair makes a similar point in his essay 'Thoughts About Empathy':

> If I know that I do not understand people and I devote all this energy and effort to figuring them out, do I have more or less empathy than people who not only do not understand me, but who do not even notice that they do not understand me?

Recent research on empathy among people with Asperger's Syndrome found that, while the cognitive aspects of understanding others' emotions (for example, knowing when someone else is upset) were difficult for them, their emotional responses were just as strong as those of non-autistic research participants. The researchers note:

> our data would suggest that when individuals with AS [Asperger's Syndrome] are given the information that allows them to understand the point of view of others, they have as much concern and compassion as unaffected [neurotypical] individuals.

Some autistic people have argued that autistic people generally have a greater empathy for animals than neurotypical people do. Certainly, Temple Grandin is famous for her understanding of cattle, although Sinclair wonders how this can be called empathy when the results of this understanding are more effective (albeit more humane) cattle slaughter systems. I don't know what to think about all of this. I'm more inclined to think that there is a big variation within both neurotypical and autistic communities. The more I read and think about autism as a concept, the more I realise how slippery it is, how much it is used to define its apparent opposite, so-called normality!

'What's the time?' asks Ben, again. I try hard not to sigh and then say, 'It's only nine thirty-five. They'll be here soon, I'm sure.'

'They'll only be a little bit late,' he says, hopefully. 'And besides, we'll have a good time.'

We're waiting for our friends at the leisure centre. I have explained to Ben that when we agree to meet at half past nine in the morning, that doesn't mean our friends will be there on the dot. There are only two of us but three of them and other people don't arrive early or on time everywhere like we do. Ben understands this and for the past week he has been debating just how late these friends will arrive, what exactly they will say to him and how they will play together in the swimming pools. About a year ago, he decided he was very keen on these two girls, daughters of my friend Bethany. Ever since then, he has thought and talked about them daily, sent them letters and cards, and made them a bead bracelet each for Christmas. He absolutely adores them and only requires that they respond to him in a positive way when we see them, which is about once every two months. I'm not sure what the big attraction is, though they are lovely girls. The strange thing is, one of these girls is the one I once saw with shock, being so much like my imaginary Alice. Ben, of course, doesn't know this and nor does Bethany or her girls, but it makes me feel much sadder when I compare his adoration of them and their demeanour to him, which is friendly but slightly wary and certainly not demonstrative.

'There they are,' says Ben, bouncing on his toes in anticipation. 'Happy New Year!' he says to them both when they are close enough.

'Hello, Ben,' says Bethany. The girls smile but don't say anything.

'Happy New Year,' says Ben again, using their names this time. There is still no reply, so I gesture to them and mouth the words. Eventually, the oldest girl catches on and says, 'Happy New Year, Ben,' and I give a sigh of relief.

They start off in the play pool, swimming around the whirlpool. The girls cling onto each other and Ben floats beside them, watching and smiling. They go down the waterslides and mess about, jumping in and out of the pool, always the girls first and Ben following. After a while the girls bump into a school friend and the three of them start playing. Ben goes off to swim in another pool for a while. When he comes back he joins in with them again, although I can see he senses that he is in some way a spare part. As he gets changed, he says to me, 'Mum, why did they play with that other girl?'

'Well, they're friendly with her, too, Ben,' I say.

'Why?' he says, sounding hurt.

'They know her from school.'

'They should go to my school. It's a better school,' he says, a statement that I am confident is not true.

After the children are dressed, we retire to the coffee shop, where Ben insists on buying (with my money) ice creams for the kids and coffee for the mums. He looks happier now that he has the girls to himself and suggests they play cards together after the ice creams, which the girls go along with. Just before we all leave, he asks, 'When will we see the girls again? In April maybe?'

'Oh, I think we could meet sooner than that,' says Bethany kindly. 'How about some time in March?'

'But how can we have an Easter-egg hunt in March?' agonises Ben. He's obviously not only planned to give the girls an Easter hunt but also established that Easter this year falls in April this year. I should probably leave him to work out how to solve the problem, but I don't; I jump in and say that I'll buy some eggs in March and we can have an early hunt.

The thing is: it breaks my heart to see how much he cares about this friendship. He enters into relationships so wholeheartedly and yet demands so little from others and treats them so gently when they unintentionally let him down. I imagine a future full of unrequited love for girls and then women who like him but don't return the full measure of his feelings.

However, he seems satisfied with his outing on the whole and is already planning the next meeting with his usual combination of optimism and anxiety.

'How many eggs will you hide? What if they don't like chocolate? What if it's a Sunday and they have to go to church instead? What if they're sick or on holiday?'

'It'll be okay, Ben,' I say, the first twenty times he asks me. Then I say firmly, 'That's enough! Turn the page,' a metaphor we've agreed upon to indicate when I feel he is falling into too much repetition (or, to put it another way, when I can't handle the same questions any more).

Ben has always liked girls more than boys. This is probably partly because girls are quieter and more verbal and he can't keep up with the sporting games that boys play. But also, there is often a little girl in school or at a park who gets interested in Ben and plays with him. 'They take a shine to me,' is how Ben puts it, and I think he's right. The only thing is, that initial 'shine' rarely turns into an ongoing friendship. I can see that all Ben's classmates like him, though they think he's weird, but not many of them can work their way around his oddities to form a close friendship with him. This year he actually got invited to two birthday parties – that's the most he's ever been to in one year.

For several years at school, Maddie was his best friend. She arrived late in the year in pre-primary and seemed slightly different from the other girls and so she latched onto Ben and made him her best friend. He happily went along with her, becoming as close to her as to any peer. Then, as Maddie got older and started fitting in more, she developed better friendships with the other girls and wanted to play with them more often. One day when they were both about eight, Ben came home and said, 'Maddie says I'm not her best friend any more. Jenna is.'

'Did she? How did you feel about that, Ben?' I asked.

'I was surprised,' he said, and I could see he was, even though everyone else in the class would have realised long ago that Maddie and Jenna were best friends.

'I expect you were sad or hurt, Ben. Or maybe jealous,' I suggested.

'No, just surprised.'

'Well,' I said, 'I'm sure Maddie is still friendly with you even if right now Jenna is her best friend. Girls do change their friends a bit.'

'Yes, I'm her second-best friend. She said.'

'Well, that's good,' I said, rather relieved. 'And who's your best friend now?'

'Maddie, of course. And Jenna is my second-best friend.'

Of course: Ben wasn't going to change his preferences just

because Maddie did. He really didn't seem hurt or jealous. And he has continued being friendly with her, even though she's gone through all the normal girl phases of powertripping and manipulating her friends, including Ben. Actually, I think Ben missed the point of most of the manipulation, just like he misses much of the petty meanness of other children. As one of his classmates once said to me, 'Whenever I say anything mean to Ben, he laughs.'

Now he's ten, he's starting to be more aware of these complex (to him) social nuances and behaviours. He can sometimes recognise that someone is saying one thing while meaning something else, but usually he takes things at face value. If the girls hadn't said 'Happy New Year' back to him at the pool, he'd have taken that as a sign they didn't like him. He could tell they played in a different way with their school friend from the way they interacted with him, but he couldn't quite work out what the difference was or what it meant. He works very hard to understand others and build friendships with his peers, but I can see how complex and difficult it is for him. As Joel Smith says, he's working in full-power translation mode all the time.

Soon after Ben was diagnosed with autism, I went to a training session run by the local autism association. After the presenter had described the classic features of autism, one of which was 'lack of theory of mind', I asked my one and only question. Can theory of mind be taught? The answer she gave was that we don't know, but her tone suggested she thought it was unlikely. At that stage, I didn't know about books like *Teaching Children with Autism How to Mind-Read* by Howlin, Baron-Cohen and Hadwin. If I had, I would probably have rushed out and bought a copy with relief. Now, I question the whole concept, especially since I read *Autism and the Myth of the Person Alone*, edited by Douglas Biklen. In this book, which is a series of interviews with autistic people (some of whom don't use verbal language) and a long introductory essay, Biklen argues that concepts such as theory of mind are metaphors scientists use to describe things they don't really understand. The notion that everyone but autistic people has a theory of mind and that therefore autism can be explained by this lack is just not proven. It's a hypothesis, but not the only one by any means, and it has been contested by researchers and by autistic self-advocates. What strikes me now is that those of us with this wonderful ability to read minds don't seem terribly good at reading the minds of autistic people, just as they make mistakes in reading neurotypical minds. Why describe this communication difference as a deficit in autistic people only?

Still, I was very anxious about the idea that Ben would go through life a solitary figure, unable to interpret those around him. (The simple idea that he would find autistic friends hadn't struck me yet.) I remember one day, we were sitting at an outside café waiting for some lunch. Ben was about four years old and at the peak of his love of numbers. Each table had an identifying number on it, and this was always slightly worrying: Ben had a tendency to go around collecting all the numbers and stockpiling them on our table so that when the waiters brought out the food chaos would reign. But on this day, Ben seemed content with a single number, which he held tightly in his hand, and all was going smoothly. Then a homeless man who generally spent his days sitting on the ground not far from the café started getting agitated, shouting out loud and pacing up and down. Ben stared at him, a little fearful.

'What's he doing?' he asked me.

'It's alright, darling,' I said. 'He's just a bit upset.'

'Why?'

'Oh, I don't know. Maybe he's having a bad day,' I replied.

'Make him stop,' demanded Ben with that touching faith in parents that children sometimes have.

'Well, darling, I can't. He's sad, you see, and I can't really change that.'

'Make him happy.'

'Oh Ben, I don't think I can make him happy. We don't know him.'

'Give him this,' suggested Ben, handing me the table number.

Immediately I thought to myself, here is evidence that my son has empathy as well as generosity! As if empathy were an object one could possess and hold onto.

Later, I told a friend about this, asking, 'Do you think Ben might have empathy after all?' She said, 'Well, what's empathy? Just telling people what they want to hear at the right time. He can learn it.'

'No,' I said. 'Surely empathy is a feeling and then what you say reflects that feeling?'

'What's the difference? Who knows what we all feel. It's what we say or do that counts.'

I have to say I was flabbergasted by this comment. She seemed a reasonably empathic person to me, but perhaps it was all just a socially acceptable way of getting through life? Did she care or just pretend?

These were the days when my experiences with Ben kept throwing a floodlight onto assumptions I had unknowingly made years ago, showing them to be unfounded or at least questionable. The ground kept moving under my feet at a time when I felt I needed to be rock solid. But I decided to trust in Ben and life on this empathy issue – to do nothing.

I'm beginning to think now that this doing-nothing approach has been one of my more successful parenting techniques!

I read: '*Sometimes Grandad and me play snap. Grandad's eyesight is on the blink so normally I win. He says, Is that a Jack of hearts? And I say, No, it's a three of spades, Grandad.* She's cheeky, isn't she?' I say to Ben.

He points to the Jack of hearts. 'I think that's a three,' he says.

'No, it's a Jack, you can see. It's just that Clarice is cheating; she wants to win.'

'Cheating!' exclaims Ben. He knows cheating is wrong. 'I think that next card is a three and she's just getting them mixed up.'

'I don't think so, Ben, I think she's tricking her grandad. She can get away with it because his eyesight isn't very good.'

Ben looks unconvinced but says, 'You can read on.'

'*Yesterday he poured a carton of soap on his cornflakes.*'

'No, Mum, soup, not soap.'

'Oh, sorry. *Soup on his cornflakes. He said, I think this milk's off. It looks a bit lumpy. I said, It's pea soup, Grandad.*' I have an image of pea soup on cornflakes and start laughing. Ben looks at my face and smiles. I laugh some more.

'You can turn the page now, Mum,' he says. But I can't because for some reason I've completely lost it now and I'm laughing like crazy, holding my stomach and bending over the book.

'Take a deep breath,' instructs Ben in a serious – or is it mock serious? – voice. I open my mouth but a huge hiccup comes out instead. The look on Ben's face makes me laugh even more.

'Take a deep breath,' he says, more firmly this time.

'Sorry, darling,' I gasp. 'I can't – *hic* – help myself.'

'I'll get a drink,' he says, running into the bathroom and filling up his own plastic cup from the sink. At the same time, I go into the kitchen and drink a teaspoon of vinegar. Then I drink Ben's glass of water, too, because I think maybe the vinegar has been in the cupboard too long; it tastes off.

'Oh dear,' I sigh, wiping my eyes.

'Now you can carry on reading,' says Ben, and we return to the couch and I continue with the story of Clarice Bean, a girl looking for peace and quiet in her own home. After Clarice causes a row with the neighbours her dad tells her she is not flavour of the month. 'Do you know what that means, Ben? Remember I told you it was a turn of phrase?'

'Not another turn of phrase,' sighs Ben.

'I know, darling, it's tricky. But do you understand?'

'I think it means she's in trouble for a month. You can read on,' says Ben, giving a sideways glance at the clock. I realise he's worried that I've wasted time laughing and he might be late for bed. There's no point me saying he can go to bed ten minutes later than usual – that doesn't suit him. He likes things to run to plan.

I finish *Clarice Bean That's Me* at 7.50 p.m. and Ben rushes off to the bathroom to do his teeth. Then we have a cuddle and talk in his bed together and at 8 p.m. we kiss goodnight.

I'm smiling as I make my after-Ben's-bedtime cup of tea, thinking about my laughter and Ben's response. Events like this made me a memoirist, because I can't let go of these small moments until I have written about them. They seem precious and meaningful. I'm wondering now why this particular experience of laughter over the book seems important to me. Is it because it's very rare for me to laugh in that full-bodied, spontaneous way? I suppose I have learned over the years to censor my emotional expressiveness because of how threatening Ben finds strong emotions, especially noisy emotions like laughter. I remember on his fourth birthday, just after the guests had left and I was feeling exhausted, something amusing happened and I fell into hysterical laughter. Ben stepped away, staring back at me with something close to horror, and turned to Robert, asking, 'What's Mum doing?' I was rather shocked then to think that he didn't know what hilarity looked like. Had he not seen me laughing like that before, I wondered. He wasn't relaxed again until I stopped laughing and he could approach me, check my face for scary stuff and then put his arms around me. It was as if he wasn't sure who I was when I was laughing. I'm happy tonight that Ben could witness me laughing and be both mildly amused and a little impatient. I want to share humour and fun with him, though what we find entertaining varies quite a lot.

I suppose I was also amused by the swapping of roles that seemed to occur. Ben did a lovely mimicry of my voice when he told me to take a deep breath. In my thinking about the future (which I don't do often), I have imagined that I might continue to take a parental role with Ben once he is an adult. I don't know what level of independence he might have and I don't think it's helpful to worry about that now, but I suppose I have imagined that he would need assistance from me or others. But this evening, I can actually imagine me at eighty-five pouring soup, or even soap, on my cornflakes and Ben pointing this out to me. Moments like these remind me to question my own assumptions about competence and independence.

Ultimately, the real value of this evening's exchange for me is its reciprocity. I want to share more of this with Ben and it feels to me as though he might want that too. When he tells me about co-prime numbers or that he has found a new swimming-pool picture on the internet, he wants me to feel the same way about these discoveries as he does. Sometimes I do: I could feel that glow of pleasure in co-primes and was able to think of an example myself (quite a challenge, but I managed). But often I don't: I just can't seem to feel anything but bored when I look at pictures of swimming pools in places I'll never visit. I cannot find it in myself to be interested in how deep the water might be and discuss this seriously – and often – with Ben as he wishes me to.

Perhaps it is neurotypicals who must rethink our ability to empathise and show reciprocity. Perhaps it is our lack of understanding of autistic people that prevents more intimacy between us. I had begun to think about this in a vague way when I came across an article by the psychologist Morton Ann Gernsbacher. She argues that if professionals, teachers and peers working with autistic children are given 'reciprocity training', then the progress made by the autistic children in language development and social engagement improves significantly. Gernsbacher says that 'reciprocity needs to be developed more purposefully by non-autistics and applied more generously to autistics', suggesting that parents imitate their autistic children's gestures and behaviour, follow the child's lead and interpret the child's behaviour as deliberate communication.

While Gernsbacher doesn't comment on any particular styles of therapy, I can see that the type of relationship-based therapy that I have been doing, on and off, with Ben for the past five years (known as DIR or 'Floortime') encourages this type of reciprocity. At the heart of this model is the idea that parents and therapists should follow a child's natural emotional interests and, through playful interaction, challenge the child towards developing their social, emotional and intellectual capacities. The approach is based on a child's particular developmental level and individual needs and is focused on building relationships and learning from these. When I think about it, it's obvious that this model of therapy is strongly reciprocal. I hadn't thought about it in this way before, probably because I don't tend to be very good about following the guidelines and usually fall back on my own intuition about what to do in any given situation. But of course my intuition has been moulded over time to be more open, to learn more from Ben and to be more reciprocal. The parenting technique of 'doing nothing' might be less about me avoiding decisions and more about me respecting Ben's desires and intentions. Sometimes following Ben's lead would result in disaster for both of us. Crossing a road, to choose a literal example, would be a fast track to the grave. But in a more metaphorical sense, to follow Ben seems sound to me. He has some sort of knack for living that I admire hugely: a way of being optimistic, making the best of things and still getting at least part of what he wants.

This optimism – the way he sees the best in everyone and starts each day with hope – has combined with Ben's generosity of spirit and humour to help develop lasting relationships with other adults in his life. Some of these people have shown tremendous empathy for Ben and have worked hard to become as close as possible to him. His aunts and uncles and cousins in particular have continually built relationships with him, even in the face of seeming rejection or lack of interest. His therapists and teachers have also demonstrated this ability to connect, both to him and to me, in meaningful and positive ways that have enriched our lives tremendously. Ben seems to bring out the best in people. I'm not sure why. I think perhaps there is a kind of innocence about him – a lack of social conditioning – that you don't often see in boys his age and that people respond to that. Or perhaps it's just his endearing personality! Whatever the reason, he and I have had ongoing support and love from family, friends and professionals. Like Ben, these people have taught me much about the art of intimacy.

It might seem ironic that mothering an autistic child has taught me about intimacy but in fact it is our differences that have pushed me further, made me learn the intricacies of this dance of connection, disconnection and reconnection that we all do all the time. This, together with my childhood as one of five siblings, has helped me develop a greater intimacy with myself as well. Those skeletons in the cupboard no longer rattle in the same way: they rest in relative tranquillity, the cupboard door always ajar.

'Mum, can I take these books to Dad's place?'

'Yes, of course, Ben. Take whatever you like.'

We're packing a box for Ben to take to Robert's place for the week of the summer holidays they are spending together. So far, there are some DVDs, a pile of books, some Christmas presents, five slinkies (coloured plastic springs), a torch and compass set, a kit to make a solar-powered car, one bag of Thomas the Tank Engines (a gesture to past interests only, I think, because otherwise he would have packed all eighty), six board games, several pens and a stack of blank paper (this latter probably just in case Dad has run out).

'Mum, I might take this game of Rummikubs to play with Dad.' Ben says this tentatively, perhaps because he remembers that I gave him that game for his last birthday, though Robert and I never worry about which things live at which house; we leave that entirely up to Ben.

'Good idea,' I reply and he balances it on the top of the box.

'Mum,' he says, 'when I get back from my week with Dad on the seventeenth, I'll play Rummikubs with you.'

'I'd like that, Ben.' I feel very moved that he imagines I might feel sad he was playing the game I chose with Dad and not with me, that he lets me know he realises this and comes up with a solution to make me feel better.

'Now,' I say, 'I think we're ready. Dad should be here soon.'

'Mum,' says Ben, 'if you miss me, you can ring me up, you know.' And he gives me a hug just as we hear Robert's car in the driveway.

THE SHAPE OF A LIFE

I will tell you a secret: a waking life is not enough for a writer. I needed a kind of parallel life to soothe me, to speak for me, to make darkness visible.—SUSAN JOHNSON

YOU WRITE YOUR LIFE as you live it. Or do you live your life as you write it?

Is there a point when writing memoir becomes your life and the pale shadowy thing other people call 'real life' is just raw material? Like waking from a powerful dream and looking about your bedroom in the half-light of dawn, you see its thinness, its weakness after the depth and saturation of your dream. The actor and her actions are not as important as the spectator and her interpretations.

It is appealing because you can perfect your memoir, in the way you cannot your life. Not that you can write perfectly – that will always elude you – but you can transform messy failed moments into delicately poised harbingers of great meaning. Pointless disagreements with your partner can become signals to the astute reader that you are, after all, destined to part. Unprovoked shouting at your son can be a message about contemporary life and the suppressed rage of the marginalised citizen. The cruel words of others can give your story conflict and sharpness. Everything has a point when you write memoir.

Or at any rate, you can give anything and everything a point with just a tweak or two. You find language for previously unnamed experiences. You create patterns, unmask meaning.

More than this, you construct a new life. And when you write memoir contemporaneously with living it, you can go far beyond the traditional reconstruction of childhood memories. You can manipulate your life as you live it.

Imagine this: I want to end my memoir with a scene where Ben and I walk down to the local park, a scene that will echo those endless walks counting letterboxes, when I was exhausted and bewildered and sometimes felt that the two of us were like members of a different species. I think it will be a neat ending to my memoir, to revisit that little park with daisies and graffiti and a broken water fountain. It will show how much (or how little) has changed. But we haven't done this recently (Ben is really too old for this park now). So, do I make it up? Of course not, that would be dishonest. But perhaps I say to him, 'Ben, let's walk down to the park today,' knowing that he is a cooperative sort of boy and will be happy to do this. And then, when we are on our way, perhaps I might say to him, 'Remember when you were four and we used to come down here all the time?' So we will talk about those times and he will probably remember something that I have forgotten. And that night, after Ben has gone to bed, I can get out my laptop and write about our walk to the park. I am telling only the truth and I remember it well because it happened only hours ago. I have engineered my neat ending.

My best memoir-writing times were sitting in cafés in West Perth while Ben attended his first therapy sessions. It wasn't worth going any further afield; parking was always difficult and I couldn't risk being late to collect Ben. I never was late, but I always imagined I might be and could see him in my mind's eye, crying in the waiting room – 'the cage' – with a nineteen-year-old therapy assistant trying to reassure him. I used to walk to a café, order coffee and cake and write in my journal. At first it was simply a debrief: 'I'm so tired,' my entries often started. Once I got into a routine, I started to record things that Ben had said or done – not milestones or therapeutic achievements, but unusual and striking things, amusing comments or behaviour I thought of as particularly Ben-like. I recorded the way he started collecting small packets of jam, honey and vegemite from a local café and then wanted to carry them everywhere, even after they became scuffed and sticky. I noted that he showed me how every power point in our local shopping centre had a number. I reproduced phrases he used, such as 'You actually don't want' and 'It's pimpling rain,' the way he touched his heart when I asked him if he knew what a treasure chest was. I tried to capture his body language when he loped in front of me at the park, picked up a stick and used it to hit different parts of the climbing frame, listening to the different sounds this made. At this stage I was just recording the things that moved or interested me. It wasn't about remembering them or sharing them. While Ben was at speech therapy, learning the correct usage of pronouns, I was at coffee-shop therapy, learning how to integrate the unexpected, worrying and puzzling aspects of motherhood.

At some point, my secret fiction-writing habit and my therapeutic journal-keeping merged, so that I stopped wanting to write and publish fiction and instead found I wanted to write memoir. I had attended a workshop as part of the Perth Writers' Festival. Sidonie Smith (an American life-writing scholar) and the Australian writer Drusilla Modjeska gave a combined seminar, followed by separate workshops. The seminar was inspiring.

Smith and Modjeska took it in turns to speak, creating a live, partially scripted dialogue. Smith walked around, her American accent projecting to the back of the room. Modjeska sat and spoke quietly into the microphone. The contrast seemed to enhance the impact of their words. I took notes in my journal (by then I never went anywhere without a soft-backed black notebook).

After the seminar, I attended Modjeska's workshop, where we wrote to some prompts she gave us and she talked about the different 'I's in memoir – the participating I, the observing I, the writing I. There was also a discussion about genre and her notion of 'fictional memoir', which is how she described her book *Poppy*. I was already a huge fan of Modjeska's work and I suddenly realised that for the past few years I had been reading more memoirs and fewer novels than ever before. It was as if my unconscious had been preparing me to write a memoir. After the workshop I asked Modjeska if she thought it was ethical to write about a child, particularly one with a disability like autism. Even at this early stage my biggest concern was about Ben's privacy. Modjeska referred to John Bayley's book *Iris* and how some people thought it was unethical or exploitative but that she felt perhaps our discomfort with the book might be more about what it depicted – for example, the scenes of bodily incontinence. I think she was suggesting that our unease with lack of control over the mind and body might be masquerading as a moral stance on privacy.

By asking that question and getting, in a sense, permission from a writer I admired, I launched myself into writing a memoir. It had to be memoir, not fiction. I knew that, in spite of the looming ethical dilemmas.

From my notebook:

Life writing is about experience and the truth of experience; about memory; about identity or subjectivity; about the creation of a narrative that weaves together these threads of someone's life.

Experience, truth, memory, identity, narrative – all of these are fundamental to memoir. And all of these are challenged by autism. Autistic people experience sensory input and perception differently from neurotypicals. The memory of an autistic person seems to work differently. Some researchers argue that autistic people have no sense of identity, that they cannot frame their life into a narrative. This is what drove me to write a memoir about my journey as Ben's mother – because autism seems to challenge so many of the assumptions that underpin our own understanding of our lives and the way we retell them to others.

In my notebook, Modjeska's question:
What is the shape of a person's life?

This question I thought about often. I thought about how the shape of my own life had seemed to change radically with the birth of my son and then again when I recognised his difference from other children his age. I wondered if his life would have a special shape because he was autistic.

Also in my notebook:
Memoir – a term encompassing the notion of meditation or reflection as well as remembrance and mourning.

I recognised that my confusion and grief required me to shape a narrative that combined my reflections on mothering with a kind of mourning for my past, my more innocent, careless self.

For over five years now, I have been writing about my experiences as a mother. While I have been writing, my son has grown from five to almost eleven years old, his father and I have separated, I have finished my doctorate, started a new job, lost friends and made new friends, visited my childhood home, published work, watched my mother recover from a stroke. I have been writing about mothering while my own mother is becoming frailer. I have been writing about parenting a child who is different from most other boys his age while I learned about what that difference meant and while he began to see those differences himself. I have been writing about autism while the Australian community has gone from near total ignorance about it to a widespread understanding of its basic features.

Over time, the writing and the living have started to fold in upon each other. I'm not sure what my life would feel like without the act of witnessing, crafting and sharing the daily moments. Writing has become so much a part of my mothering role, how can I relinquish it? How will I understand my own life and treasure my son's life if I don't write about it? Many people have written about the impossibility of memoir – its unseemliness, vulgarity, narcissism, betrayals – but where is the literature on the impossibility of life *without* memoir?

Paradoxically, writing memoir relies more on forgetting than remembering. In order to write about events or experiences that are meaningful, you have to release all of the other moments that you don't write about. I think back over the past ten years. About our crumpled crying baby who didn't know how to suck or sleep. About the toddler with a rigid body and stony face, sitting on his own in a room full of laughing, playing children. The child mesmerised by the alphabet, terrified by noises, trying to pull smells out of his mouth. All the doctors and their tests and questions, the therapists with their advice and instructions. The one hundred books on autism I have read. I think of toilet training and load after load of washing in winter. Of red wine all over the kitchen floor, a river running out of the bathroom, the broken window in the laundry. Meetings at the school, explaining, negotiating, urging. The obsessions with numbers, Bananas in Pyjamas, drains, toilet flush buttons, swimming pools, dinosaurs, Mr Men characters, frogs, Thomas the Tank Engines, measuring tapes, thermometers. Long walks reading letterboxes. Endless conversations about numbers and trains and swimming pools. Doubts and confusion, decisions I've had to make without adequate information. I think about all the injuries I have done to Ben, all the things I insisted he must do: swing, go down slides, go to the dentist, have a haircut, attend childcare, learn to swim, have a blood test, interact with other children. I think about the hard things I've had to tell Ben: that he's autistic, that he needs extra help, that he is different from his peers. I think about those four months of depression the year after his diagnosis, when just getting through the day was a struggle. I think about the long road out of that place.

All these things happened. Some I have written about.

I think also about how every morning Ben wakes up happy and optimistic. His amazing courage and enthusiasm for life. How he loves school and learning. How many people he has won over with his politeness, humour and affection. Little things he says that are so characteristic, like asking me, 'When I eat crisps, do I look chic?' or saying that for breakfast he had 'toast and mushrooms under salt'. I worry I haven't been able to convey his deeper, more thoughtful side – how at four he said, 'I was born in space in the dark' and at eight we had many conversations about death and the mechanics of how the dead, once buried, could reach heaven or be reincarnated.

I wonder if I have communicated the complex and unusual boy he has become and how his view of the world has changed me. All my life, I've been missing things that Ben has shown me

– the shape of shells, the number of petals on flowers, the colour of swimming pools, the different types of clouds, the way some words have no antonyms, the number of words that are spelled in three different ways in English, the different fonts used in children's picture books, the fact that people lie to one another all the time, why it is that bullying thrives, our daily acceptance of malice.

Jane Smiley notes that 'one of the trials of intimacy with a writer' is 'to be observed in detail'. But is it always a trial to be observed so closely? Perhaps it can also be a gift to be watched with interest and compassion by someone who loves us. To watch your own child so closely is a privilege but, as most parents know, also at times a shocking experience. Your fond notions of how important you are to the child, the good grounding you gave him in cultural matters, the disdain for material possessions, the sceptical but compassionate view of the world you passed on to him – these may be more projections than realities.

Because he seemed at times so different from me, so puzzling to me, I have observed Ben very closely all his life. And because he recognises that other people are confusing and cannot be taken at face value, Ben observes me rather closely. We allow each other some privacy – we have secrets from each other – but we are a little knowing about these secrets.

'Why are you doing a sneaky smile?' asked Ben the other day.

'I'm smiling because you are smiling in a cheeky way,' I replied. 'I think you might be about to do something naughty!'

'Mum!' he protested, trying not to laugh, his face alight with the prospect of breaking one of our minor house rules. (Or so I thought: later I discovered he had already played his trick on me – swapping the knobs of the salt and pepper grinders.)

*

I have started reading sections of my memoir to Ben. Like all children, he loves to hear stories about his own past. Because he also loves reading and writing, he understands that some of my writing includes him, using the name Ben, not his real name. The scenes I read to him are all moments that I think he will enjoy, for example the time when he was two and didn't want to swing or play in the sandpit but enjoyed being inside a cave. Not long ago, I read Ben the scene where Robert and I were trying to enforce our rule that he couldn't talk about numbers while at dinner. Ben loved it. He fell about laughing and asked me to give him a copy to read himself. After he'd reread it, we talked about why we'd tried to stop him talking about numbers all the time. Then he said, 'Mum, it's good that I don't spit rice on the table any more and run away, isn't it?'

'Yes,' I said, 'it is good. And it's also good that we talk about all sorts of things at dinner now, isn't it?' He didn't reply but looked at me through suddenly narrowed eyes.

Later that day, as we sat down to our dinner together, he gave me a sly grin and said, 'Mum, did you know there is something called the Fibonacci series? I'll tell you about it.' And he insisted I listen to a sequence of numbers and how they are calculated.

I see this as his way of re-interpreting my writing. At one level, he is now old enough to accept that not everyone loves numbers (or whatever his current interest is) and that if he wants good relationships, he needs to be able to discuss things other than his latest passion. On another level, it is clear that he is telling me that he is not going to give up his interest in numbers just to please me, nor is he buying into the idea that the superficial and generalist interests of neurotypicals are superior to the highly specialised interests of autistic people.

He isn't yet challenging the way I have represented him. But I expect he will. In fact, I hope he will. Writing a memoir about a mother–son relationship while living that relationship was always going to be tricky, not just in terms of ethics but also on questions of 'truth', on how the interactions between us can justifiably be interpreted. Since my starting premise was the idea of difference, it seems appropriate that Ben's understanding of our relationship will not only be different from my own but will also involve a critique and reconstruction of my interpretations. Whether he'll ever do this through writing, I don't know, but I can see he is already doing so through living.

There is another challenge in writing about mothering when your son is still young, and that is how to end your memoir. I don't want to predict Ben's future, because that isn't my role. Ben will determine his own future. I have no advice for other parents, no words of wisdom to end on. So I have to fall back on my old strategy – the question.

'Ben, if you were writing a story about your life so far, like a book, how would you end it?' I ask him.

'How many pages would it have?' he replies.

This is such a typical response, I smile. 'Oh, I don't know. Three hundred, maybe.'

He frowns slightly and then corrects me. 'I think it will be 220 pages, like that Morris Gleitzman book we've just finished reading.'

'Okay, yes, 220 pages would be good. So, how would you end it?'

'Page 150 would probably be when you decided to move me from my old school to my new school. Page 220 would be that I'm settling in very well.'

'That's a good ending, Ben,' I say. 'Do you mind if I write that down?'

'No, Mum, I don't mind,' he says.

And so I do.

ACKNOWLEDGEMENTS

Earlier versions of the following chapters have been published elsewhere and I gratefully acknowledge the input of the editors of these journals:

'On Pomegranates and Life Stories' in *Indigo*, 3 (2009): 32–7.

'Reaching One Thousand' in *Australian Book Review*, 298 (2008): 32–8.

'Bonus' in *Griffith Review*, 22 (2008): 147–55.

'Geometry of Echoes' in *Westerly*, 55.2 (2010): 211–27.

'Carving, Forging, Stealing' in *Life Writing*, 7.3 (2010): 305–19.

I am also grateful to Syracuse University Press and the editors for permission to re-use several paragraphs from the following book chapter: 'Sharing Stories: Motherhood, Autism and Culture' by Rachel Robertson, from *Disability and Mothering: Liminal Spaces of Embodied Knowledge*, edited by Cynthia Lewiecki-Wilson and Jen Cellio (Syracuse University Press, Syracuse, New York, 2011).

*

I have been fortunate to receive support and encouragement from many people, both in parenting my son and in writing this book about mothering.

An early version of this book formed part of a doctoral thesis at Curtin University and I am grateful to the School of Media, Culture and Creative Arts and to my supervisor, Julienne van

Loon. Thank you also to my colleagues Mary Besemeres, Liz Byrski, Tim Dolin and David Whish-Wilson for their advice and support. My thanks go to all the staff at Black Inc., especially editor Denise O'Dea.

Friends have been generous with their support; thank you in particular to Gill Faller, Elizabeth Farmer, Lynn Gauntlett, Karen Rickman, Anna Sabadini, Rosemary Stevens and Annamaria Weldon.

I thank Sharon Campbell, Robin Jones, Michelle Marsh, Kathy Walmsley and John Wray for their wisdom and guidance, and Nancy Giglia and Fiona Munro for their insightful assistance. Rose Marks and Jacqueline McManus are like fairy godmothers – their loving support has made a huge contribution to our lives.

My family are extraordinary; they have provided years of emotional, practical and financial support to me and my son. My deepest gratitude goes to my parents, my siblings and their partners, and my nieces and nephews. My family has been generous in allowing me to write about some of our shared experiences, although I have tried to respect their privacy. Whilst they don't appear very often in this book, they are very strong presences in our lives.

I thank 'Robert' for his commitment to our son and our joint parenting.

Most of all, I am deeply grateful to my son (called 'Ben' in these pages), the inspiration for this book. With his characteristic affection and generosity, he has allowed me to write about our relationship. Just by being himself, he gives so much.

NOTES

On Pomegranates and Life Stories: an Introduction

1   *The real is not given to us*: Einstein, Albert. 'Reply to Criticisms'. *Albert Einstein: Philosopher Scientist*. Edited by Paul A. Schilpp. Cambridge: Cambridge University Press, 1949, p. 680.

1   *As a piece of a pomegranate*: Song of Solomon 6:7. The Bible, authorised King James Version. Introduction and notes by Robert Carroll and Stephen Prickett. Oxford: Oxford University Press, 1998, p. 50.

4   *Loose photographs you can shuffle*: Polizzotto, Carolyn. *Pomegranate Season*. Fremantle: Fremantle Arts Centre Press, 1998.

6   *About the pomegranate I must say nothing*: Pausanias. *Description of Greece* 2.17.4. Translated by W.H.S. Jones. The Theoi Project, http://www.theoi.com, accessed 27 December 2010.

Reaching One Thousand

7   *I have often admired the mystical way*: Browne, Sir Thomas. *Religio Medici* (1643). Great Literature Online, http://browne.classicauthors.net/ReligioMedici, accessed 27 December 2010.

16   *The presence of odd family members*: Siegel, Bryna. *The World of the Autistic Child*. Oxford: Oxford University Press, 1996, p. 92.

16   *research has shown*: Baron-Cohen, Simon et al. 'Autism occurs more often in families of physicists, engineers and mathematicians,' *Autism* 2 (1998): 296–301.

17   *The American diagnostic bible on 'mental disorders'*: American Psychiatric Association. *Diagnostic and Statistical Manual of Mental Disorders*, 4th edition (*DSM IV*). Washington, DC: American Psychiatric Association, 1994.

23   *lack the ability to see 'the big picture', to integrate things and make sense of the world. Their ability to shift attention is also impaired*: These are the weak central coherence and executive function theories respectively. See Frith, Uta. *Autism: Explaining the Enigma*, 2nd edition. Oxford: Blackwell, 2003.

23   *an extreme form of the 'male' or systematising brain*: Baron-Cohen, Simon. *The Essential Difference: Men, Women and the Extreme Male Brain*. London: Penguin Books, 2004.

24   *etymology of the word integer*: *Oxford Dictionary of English*, 2nd edition. Oxford: Oxford University Press, 2010. Accessed online, http://www.oed.com, 27 December 2010.

25   *Evidence for the human capacity for counting*: Butterworth, Brian. *What Counts: How Every Brain Is Hardwired for Math*. New York: Simon & Schuster, 1990.

25   *the intimate architecture of the world*: Szatmari, Peter. *A Mind Apart: Understanding Children with Autism and Asperger Syndrome*. New York: Guildford Press, 2004, p. 15.

25   *There are moments, as I'm falling into sleep*: Tammet, Daniel. *Born on a Blue Day: A Memoir of Asperger's and an Extraordinary Mind*. London: Hodder and Stoughton, 2006, pp. 9–10.

Raw Experience

29   *What sweet Contentments doth the Soul*: Drummond, William. *The Works of William Drummond, of Hawthorden*. Edinburgh, 1711. Google Books, www.books.google.com.au, accessed 27 December 2010.

33   *Bryna Siegel explains*: Siegel, Bryna. *The World of the Autistic Child*. Oxford: Oxford University Press, 1996.

35   *In Buddhist cultures*: Classen, Constance. *Worlds of Sense: Exploring the senses in history and across culture*. New York: Routledge, 1993.

36   *In her book* Worlds of Sense: Classen, *Worlds of Sense*.

36   *In parts of India, smelling the head*: Classen, *Worlds of Sense*, p. 99.

42   *Diane Ackerman's book*: Ackerman, Diane. *A Natural History of the Senses*. New York: Vintage Books, 1990, p. 308.

43   *Classen suggests that smell is 'by nature of great importance'*: Classen, *Worlds of Sense*, p. 45.

44   *Oliver Sacks argues*: Sacks, Oliver. *The Man Who Mistook His Wife for a Hat*. London: Pan Macmillan, 1985.

The Blank Face

48   *The awful thing is that beauty*: Dostoyevsky, Fyodor. *The Brothers Karamazov*. Translated by Constance Garnett. New York: Random House, 1995, p. 118.

52   *When we call someone a genius*: Nazeer, Kamran. *Send in the Idiots: Stories from the other side of autism*. London: Bloomsbury, 2006, p. 81.

52   *Doreen Virtue*: Virtue, Doreen. 'Indigo, Crystal and Rainbow Children', AngelTherapy.com, http://www.angeltherapy. com/article1.php. Accessed 1 December 2011. See also her books *The Care and Feeding of Indigo Children* (Hay House, 2001) and *The Crystal Children* (Hay House, 2003).

53   *Other people want to protect them*: Nazeer, *Send in the Idiots*, p. 159.

56   *Cat balloon did not hear their loud cries*: Morgan, Palo. *Cat Balloon*. Fremantle, Fremantle Arts Centre Press, 1992.

58   *'cure or kill' approach*: Couser, G. Thomas. *Vulnerable Subjects: Ethics and life writing*. Ithaca: Cornell University Press, 2004, p. 150.

58   *Elspeth Probyn suggests*: Probyn, Elspeth. *Blush: Faces of Shame*. Sydney: University of NSW Press, 2005.

58   *Probyn quotes Gerhardt Piers*: Probyn, *Blush*, p. 3.

61   Insight *program*: 'Understanding Autism', *Insight*, SBS Television, 8 August 2006. Online transcript, http://www.sbs. com.au/insight/archive, accessed 20 May 2007.

62   *Cure Autism Now and Autism Speaks*: Cure Autism Now and Autism Speaks merged in 2007. See http://www.autismspeaks. org.

63   *Aspies for Freedom, for example, say*: Aspies for Freedom, http:// www.aspiesforfreedom.com, accessed 20 May 2007.

63   *I am not a puzzle*: Harrison, David and Tony Freinberg. 'Autistic Liberation Front fights the "oppressors searching for a cure"',

The Telegraph (UK), 1 September 2005. Online at http://www.aspiesforfreedom.com/showthread.php?tid=733, accessed 20 May 2007.

Winding

65   *We are brought out of darkness*: *The Book of Common Prayer and Administration of Sacraments*. London, 1660, p. 160. Google Books, accessed 27 December 2010.

66   *The* Oxford English Dictionary *offers*: Oxford University Press. *Oxford Dictionary of English*. Accessed online, 30 June 2008.

68   *In his 1967 book* The Empty Fortress: Bettelheim, Bruno. *The Empty Fortress: Infantile Autism and the Birth of the Self*. New York: Simon & Schuster, 1967.

68   *According to Richard Pollack*: Pollack, Richard D. *The Creation of Dr B: A Biography of Bruno Bettelheim*. Rockfeller Centre: Touchstone, 1997.

69   *Even after the psychogenic approach to autism*: Grinker, Roy Richard. *Unstrange Minds: A Father Remaps the World of Autism*. Cambridge: Icon Books, 2008, p. 97.

75   *In 1997, Richard Pollack published*: Pollack, *The Creation of Dr B*.

76   *Writing about Paul Celan's poem*: Pollack, *The Creation of Dr B*, p. 143.

The Cage

80   *The eyes of others our prisons*: Woolf, Virginia. 'An Unwritten Novel'. *Monday or Tuesday*. Project Gutenberg Australia, March 2002, http://gutenberg.net.au/ebooks02/0200211.txt, accessed 27 December 2010.

89   *I have been reading* Out of Africa: Blixen, Karen. *Out of Africa*. London: Putnam, 1937, pp. 269–70.

92   *Telling an interrupted life requires*: Frank, Arthur W. *The Wounded Storyteller: Body, Illness and Ethics*. Chicago: University of Chicago Press, 1995, p. 58.

92   *The 'wreckage' Frank discusses* : Frank, *The Wounded Storyteller*, p. 60 .

Bonus

94   *Too many have dispensed with*: Albert Camus quoted in *The International Thesaurus of Quotations*. Edited by Rhonda Thomas Tripp. Cromwell, 1970. Google Books, accessed 27 December 2010.

95   *The term bonus was originally*: Oxford University Press. *Oxford Dictionary of English*. Accessed online, 30 June 2008.

95   *Carer is a recently coined word*: Oxford University Press. *Oxford Dictionary of English*. Accessed online, 30 June 2008.

97   *I am reminded here of the French philosopher Louis Althusser*: Althusser, Louis. *Lenin and Philosophy and Other Essays*. Translated by Ben Brewster. New York and London: Monthly Review Press, 1971.

99   *In her book* Ordinary Time, *Nancy Mairs says*: Mairs, Nancy. *Ordinary Time: Cycles in marriage, faith and renewal*. Boston: Beacon Press, 1993, p. 214.

101 *The disability scholar Robert Murphy*: Murphy, Robert F. *The Body Silent*. New York: WW Norton, 1990.

102 *What Michael Bérubé calls*: Bérubé, Michael. *Life as We Know It*. New York: Pantheon, 1996, p. 13.

102 *Liminality, of course, may also be*: Turner, Victor. *The Forest of Symbols: Aspects of Ndembu Ritual*. Ithaca: Cornell University Press, 1967.

Geometry of Echoes

105 *And always, in our daydreams*: Bachelard, Gaston. *The Poetics of Space*. Translated by Maria Jolas. Boston: Beacon Press, 1994, p. 7.

108 *Is it, as Edward Relph, says*: Relph, Edward. *Place and Placelessness*. London: Pion, 1976, p. 39.

109 *When Simone Weil declares*: Weil, Simone. *The Need for Roots*. Translated by Arthur Wills. New York: Harper & Row, 1952, p. 43.

113 *Our house is our corner of the world*: Bachelard, *The Poetics of Space*, p. 4.

113 *The house of our childhood is*: Bachelard, *The Poetics of Space*, p. 15.

120 *We do not have to be long in the woods*: Bachelard, *The Poetics of Space*, p. 185.

120 *If the house is what Bachelard calls*: Bachelard, *The Poetics of Space*, p. 60.

120 *As Mary Pershall describes it*: Pershall, Mary. 'A Home Away from Home'. *Inner Cities: Australian women's memory of place*. Edited by Drusilla Modjeska. Ringwood: Penguin, 1989, pp. 111–17.

Carving, Forging, Stealing

123 *Writers are natural murderers.*: Freed, Lynn. *Reading, Writing and Leaving Home: Life on the page*. Orlando, Florida: Harcourt Books, 2005, p. 30.

133 *In* Secrets, *Sissela Bok defines*: Bok, Sissela. *Secrets: On the ethics of concealment and revelation*. New York: Vintage, 1983, p. 10.

133 *She says: 'Claims to privacy ...'*: Bok, *Secrets*, p. 11.

133 *Bok points out that 'unwarranted access ...'*: Bok, *Secrets*, p. 27.

134 *Bok argues in favour of*: Bok, *Secrets*, p. 27.

134 *This is really about power*: Bok, *Secrets*, p. 282.

136 *Paul John Eakin suggests that*: Eakin, Paul John. *How Our Lives Become Stories: Making selves*. Ithaca: Cornell University Press, 1999, p. 186.

136 *Sidonie Smith suggests that*: Smith, Sidonie. 'Identity's Body'. *Autobiography and Postmodernism*. Edited by Kathleen Ashley, Leigh Gilmore and Gerald Peters. Boston: University of Massachusetts, 1994, pp. 266–92.

137 *She describes this as a form of 'pathological ruthlessness'*: Freed, Lynn. *Reading, Writing and Leaving Home*, p. 38.

Pumpkin Scones

140 *School's a weird thing*: Depp, Johnny. Quoted on *Thinkexist.com*. Accessed 27 December 2010.

158 *Gail Landsman has argued that*: Landsman, Gail. 'Does God Give Special Kids to Special Parents?: Personhood and the Child with Disabilities as Gift and as Giver'. *Transformative Motherhood: On giving and getting in a consumer culture*. Edited

by Linda L. Layne. New York: New York University Press, 1999: pp. 133–65.

160 *According to Robert Weiss*: Weiss, R.S. *Loneliness: the experience of emotional and social isolation.* Cambridge: MIT Press, 1973.

161 *I have seen research that suggests*: Bauminger, Nirit and Connie Kasari. 'The Experience of Loneliness and Friendship in Autism'. *The Research Basis for Autism Intervention.* Edited by Eric Schopler et al. New York: Klumer Academic, 2001, pp. 151–69. Bauminger, Nirit, Cory Shulman and Galit Agam. 'Peer Interaction and Loneliness in High-Functioning Children with Autism'. *Journal of Autism and Developmental Disorders,* 3.5 (2003): 489–507.

161 *As Heinrich Pestalozzi said*: Pestalozzi, Heinrich. Quoted in Miller, Alice. *The Drama of Being a Child.* Translated by Ruth Ward. London: Virago, 1987, p. 52.

Frog in Girlland

162 *There is no greater agony*: Angelou, Maya. Quoted in Britt, Rugen. *Black and Powerful: A career guide for tomorrow's top leaders.* Airleaf Publishing, 2008. Google Books, accessed 27 December 2010, http://books.google.com.au.

166 *series of stories by Arnold Lobel*: Arnold Lobel's Frog and Toad books are *Frog and Toad Are Friends* (1970), *Frog and Toad Together* (1972), *Frog and Toad All Year* (1976) and *Days with Frog and Toad* (1979), all published in New York by Harper Collins.

168 *one of the diagnostic criteria*: American Psychiatric Association. *Diagnostic and Statistical Manual of Mental Disorders (DSM IV).*

169 *I found myself reading a research paper*: Low, Jason, Elizabeth Goddard and Joseph Melser. 'Generativity and Imagination in Autism Spectrum Disorder: Evidence from individual differences in children's impossible entity drawings'. *British Journal of Developmental Psychology,* 27.2 (2009): 425–44.

169 *Oliver Sacks compares*: Sacks, Oliver. *An Anthropologist on Mars.* London: Pan Macmillan, 1995, p. 275.

169 *Similarly, we enacted many times the moment*: Grahame, Kenneth.

The Wind in the Willows. Oxford, Oxford University Press, 1983, p. 32.

170 *biscuits, potted lobster, sardines*: Grahame, *The Wind in the Willows*, p. 19.

170 *As disabled dancer Neil Marcus*: Marcus, Neil. Quoted in Levin, Mike. 'The Art of Disability: An interview with Tobin Siebers'. *Disability Studies Quarterly*, 30.2 (2010): n.p. Accessed online, 27 December 2010, http://www.dsq-sds.org/article/view/1263/1272.

170 *Tito Mukhopadhyay, an autistic poet*: Mukhopadhyay, Tito Rajarshi. 'Questions and Answers'. *Autism and the Myth of the Person Alone*. Douglas Biklen et al. New York: New York University Press, 2005, p. 120.

171 *two theories about autism*: On weak central coherence theory see Frith, Uta. *Autism: Explaining the Enigma*. 2ⁿᵈ edition. Oxford: Blackwell, 2003. On theory of mind see Baron-Cohen, Simon. *Mindblindness: An essay on autism and theory of mind*. Cambridge: MIT Press, 1995.

171 *Bruce Mills has argued*: Mills, Bruce. 'Autism and Imagination'. *Autism and Representation*. Edited by Mark Osteen. New York: Routledge, 2008, pp. 117–32.

172 *Oliver Sacks (agreeing with Coleridge)*: Sacks, *An Anthropologist on Mars*, pp. 230–1.

176 *In his book* How Our Lives Become Stories: Eakin, *How Our Lives Become Stories*, p. 123.

176 *In his work with people with neurological damage*: Sacks, *The Man Who Mistook His Wife for a Hat*, p. 105.

176 *Sidonie Smith, for example*: Smith, Sidonie. 'Taking It to a Limit One More Time: Autobiography and Autism'. *Getting A Life: Everyday uses of autobiography*. Edited by Sidonie Smith and Julia Watson. Minneapolis: University of Minnesota Press, 1996, pp. 226–46.

177 *Developmental psychologists have shown*: See for example Siegel, Daniel. *The Developing Mind*. New York: Guilford Press, 1999.

177 *Eakin argues that the development of*: Eakin, *How Our Lives Become Stories*, p. 123.

177 *It was as if he had no notion of*: On the private self and other types of self, see Neisser, Ulrich. 'Concepts and Self-concepts'. *The Conceptual Self in Context: Culture, experience, self-understanding.* Edited by Ulrich Neisser and David Jopling. Cambridge: Cambridge University Press, 1997.

Fancy Footwork

181 *The meeting of two personalities*: Jung, Carl G. *Modern Man in Search of a Soul.* Abingdon, Oxon: Routledge Classics, 2001, pp. 49–50.

185 *Jim Sinclair, an autistic rights activist, says*: Sinclair, Jim. 'Bridging the Gaps: an Inside-Out View of Autism (or, Do You Know What I Don't Know?)'. *High-Functioning Individuals with Autism.* Edited by Eric Schopler and Gary B. Mesibov. New York: Plenum Press, 1992, pp. 294–302.

185 *My selfhood is undamaged*: Sinclair, 'Bridging the Gaps', pp. 294–302.

186 *SavedAspie says*: Posted response to 'Autism and Empathy' post, 4 April 2009. Accessed online, http://aspie-bird.blogspot.com/2009/04/autism-and-empathy-grief-about-missing.html, 27 December 2010.

187 *theory of mind*: See Baron-Cohen, Simon. *Mindblindness.*

187 *Joel Smith says*: Smith, Joel. Blog entry, accessed 10 June 2009, but this post is now archived. Joel Smith's current blog is at http://thiswayoflife.org/index.html, accessed 9 November 2011.

188 *Jim Sinclair makes a similar point*: Sinclair, Jim. 'Thoughts About Empathy'. Jim Sinclair, http://web.archive.org/web/20090321213935/http://web.syr.edu/~jisincla/empathy.htm, accessed 9 November 2011.

188 *Recent research on empathy*: Rogers, Kimberley et al. 'Who Cares? Revisiting Empathy in Asperger's Syndrome'. *Journal of Autism and Developmental Disorders*, 37 (2007): 709–15, p. 713.

188 *although Sinclair wonders how this can be called*: Sinclair, Jim. 'If you love something, you don't kill it'. Jim Sinclair, http://

web.archive.org/web/20081020061906/http://web.syr.
edu/~jisincla/killing.htm, accessed 9 November 2011.

193 *books like* Teaching Children with Autism How to Mind-Read:
Howlin, Patricia, Simon Baron-Cohen and Julie Hadwin.
*Teaching Children with Autism How to Mind-Read: A Practical
Guide.* Chichester: John Wiley & Sons, 1999.

194 *I read* Autism and the Myth of the Person Alone: Douglas
Biklen et al. *Autism and the Myth of the Person Alone.* New York:
New York University Press, 2005.

196 *I read: 'Sometimes Grandad and me play snap ...':* Child, Lauren.
Clarice Bean That's Me. London: Orchard Books, 1999.

199 *Gernsbacher says that*: Gernsbacher, Morton Ann. 'Toward a
Behavior of Reciprocity'. *Journal of Developmental Processes*, 1.1
(2006): 139–52, Accessed online 10 June 2009, http://psych.
wisc.edu/lang/pdf/gernsbacher_reciprocity.pdf, p. 141.

199 *DIR or 'Floortime'*: The DIR model (which encompasses 'Floortime') was developed by Stanley Greenspan and Serena
Wieder. See the Interdisciplinary Council on Developmental
and Learning Disorders website, www.icdl.com, accessed 10
June 2009.

The Shape of a Life

203 *I will tell you a secret*: Johnson, Susan. *A Better Woman: A memoir.*
Sydney: Random House, 1999, p. 86.

206 *her book* Poppy: Modjeska, Drusilla. *Poppy.* Melbourne: Penguin
Books, 1990.

206 *John Bayley's book* Iris: Bayley, John. *Iris: A memoir of Iris Murdoch.*
London: Gerald Duckworth & Co, 1998.

210 *Jane Smiley notes*: Smiley, Jane. 'A Reluctant Muse Embraces
His Task, and Everything Changes'. *Writers on Writing: Collected
Essays from The New York Times.* Introduction by John Darnton.
New York: Times Books, 2002, p. 219.

CPSIA information can be obtained
at www.ICGtesting.com
Printed in the USA
LVHW082341110719
623865LV00009BA/432/P

9 781863 955553